COMPANION TO THE
GOOD NEWS OLD TESTAMENT

Joseph Rhymer was born in 1927 and holds degrees in Philosophy from Leeds University and Theology from Edinburgh University. After some years as an Anglican priest and member of the Community of the Resurrection he entered the Roman Catholic Church in 1963 and is now on the staff of Notre Dame College of Education, Glasgow. Author of a number of books on the Bible and on Religious Education, he is perhaps best known for his editing of the monumental *The Bible in Order*. He is deeply involved in international and inter-church co-operation for helping people to understand the Bible.

Anthony Bullen, from 1964 to 1975, was Director of Religious Education for the Archdiocese of Liverpool, England. As Director he was responsible for a programme of religious studies for children from Kindergarten to High School – a programme in use in many parts of the world. He is the author of a number of books for religious teachers and activity-booklets for children. During the last decade he has been in constant dialogue with parents, teachers and children over the subject of religious education. He is now Pastor of a busy parish in Liverpool.

Companion to the
Good News
Old Testament

JOSEPH RHYMER AND
ANTHONY BULLEN

Collins
FONTANA BOOKS

First published in Fontana Books, 1976

© Joseph Rhymer and Anthony Bullen, 1976

THE GOOD NEWS BIBLE OLD TESTAMENT
(Today's English Version)
© American Bible Society 1976

Made and printed in Great Britain by
William Collins Sons & Co Ltd Glasgow

CONTENTS

Contents

INTRODUCTION

This is a book for explorers, a guide to the fascinating world of the Old Testament.

It is a world inhabited by people with experiences we will recognize as our own, and with religious insights which illuminate the situations and problems faced by every generation.

They are people who dance at weddings, sing with joy and thanksgiving at harvest time, help the bereaved and unfortunate, and confront their enemies.

They tell their children the old, familiar stories about the great days of the past. They struggle to grasp new and frightening situations as they are caught in the turmoil of international forces.

The smoke of their burning homes rises behind them as they are herded away to exile and slavery. Their grandchildren return to build new cities from the old ruins and to start new lives.

Religion is woven into the very fabric of their lives. God is a dynamic, living, relevant presence to them. They grow to know him, as they themselves grow to maturity as a people. These people speak for themselves, and speak to us, in the pages of the Old Testament. This present book aims to remove the obscurities which prevent us from hearing them clearly.

There are articles about the way these people thought, the historical events which affected them so deeply, and about the part of the world where they lived out their lives.

The origins of Jerusalem and the Temple are described, and the everyday life of ordinary Hebrew citizens and country folk. Their religious beliefs are explained, and the ways in which they expressed their beliefs in worship.

Introduction

There is a dictionary of words and expressions which might be puzzling to a modern reader (chapter 10). Each book of the Old Testament is provided with a brief commentary and with suggestions about the best way to read it. Commentaries are also provided for the additional books which are included in some other editions of the Old Testament.

In these pages, we only want to open windows and doors into the world of the Old Testament, so that the reader can see how attractive it is.

Once people begin to feel at home in it they no longer need a guide book. In fact this book will have served its purpose best when the reader feels that he or she no longer needs it.

Part One

THE BACKGROUND
TO THE OLD TESTAMENT

Chapter 1

LANDS AND PEOPLES OF
THE OLD TESTAMENT

We are all of us deeply affected by the places where we are born, are nurtured and live out our lives. Many factors went into the making of the Hebrews of the Old Testament, but one of the strongest forces to shape them was the area of the world in which they lived.

Palestine is a corridor country, a passage which connects the two main areas of the Middle East. This has only changed comparatively recently since the Suez Canal was cut, and the development of air transport has altered the communication patterns of the world.

There is a simple reason for the importance of Palestine in ancient times. The Middle East is dominated by two great river valleys which have been cradles of civilization from the earliest times for which we have any evidence. Palestine connects them.

Egypt

In the south the river Nile rises in the lakes of central Africa and the mountains of Ethiopia, and flows northward through the desert until it reaches the Mediterranean Sea in a sprawling swamp of river mouth and marshes. For a great part of its journey, the river cuts through one of the bleakest areas upon earth.

In places the fertile, cultivated strip along its banks is no more than a mile across from waste sand to waste sand, and the narrow ribbon of green demands ceaseless labour with irrigation channels to carry the precious water on to the land.

Yet the people who drained the marshes of the Nile and dug the channels, formed one of the greatest civilizations the world has known. The Pyramids were already ancient when Abraham visited Egypt.

The river Nile was the back-bone of Egypt, and its main god. Its water, and the mud left behind when the river returned to its channel after the annual floods, turned the desert into rich agricultural land. The river was the only means of communication between the broad fertile lands near the Mediterranean coast and Upper Egypt, a thousand miles up the Nile.

No wonder that Egypt was the granary of the ancient Middle East. No matter how severe the famine might be in the area, the waters of the Nile guaranteed the crops of Egypt.

Mesopotamia

At the other end of the Middle East, north and west of Palestine, another great river complex, the Tigris and Euphrates, formed another ancient cradle of civilizations.

The Greeks named it 'the land between the rivers', Mesopotamia, and so it has remained. A mountain barrier divides it from India. A succession of great empires rose and fell in Mesopotamia as first one group and then another gained control.

At the time of Abraham, when the Hebrews first appeared on the scene, no single state dominated Mesopotamia. In the deep south the town of Ur was the most important settlement, and it was from Ur that Abraham's family set out on their momentous journey towards Canaan, or Palestine, as it was later to be called.

Nearly a thousand years later the Assyrians gained control of the whole area and created the first great empire in the Middle East. They in their turn were defeated by the Babylonians in 612 BC, and the Babylonians by the Persians a mere seventy years later.

The last people to rule the whole Middle East were the Greeks under the leadership of Alexander, who gave his name to so many cities in the area. But by then the centre of political power was moving to Rome and Mesopotamia faded into insignificance.

Palestine, the Corridor Country

There was no direct route between Mesopotamia and Egypt, because the two areas are separated by hundreds of miles of impassable desert. At various times caravan routes have been established across it. But the main international road has always had to skirt the desert via Damascus in the north, and then strike south to the coast; or pass along the eastern side of the deep trench in which the river Jordan and the Dead Sea lie.

Palestine occupies the narrow corridor flanked to the west by the Mediterranean Sea and to the east by the Syrian desert, with the main international routes passing through it. Great powers fought each other for control of this vital area.

Soldiers, traders and the officials of successive conquerors exposed the Hebrews to a wide range of foreign influences. The effects are to be seen in every aspect of their national life: in government, law, religion and in the very language spoken by the people.

In time these foreign influences provoked in the Hebrew people a strong religious reaction. Thus a tension runs deeply in the Old Testament between Hebrew exclusiveness on the one hand, and, on the other hand, the Hebrew consciousness of a vocation to bring the whole world to God.

Neighbours of the Hebrews

The Hebrews shared Palestine and its immediate surroundings with other groups of peoples who formed small states, similar to the Hebrew nation and equally insignificant in the eyes of the great powers of the times.

On the Mediterranean coast towards Egypt, the seaborne invaders called the Philistines established a loose federation of five cities. To the north lay the Lebanon with its seafaring traders, and the Syrians of Damascus. Three states occupied the eastern heights of the Jordan valley: Ammon, Moab and Edom, to complete the circle of neighbouring countries.

For a brief period during the reigns of David and Solomon the Hebrews managed to establish control over the whole of this small area. But the small states quickly established their independence, and there was often bitter enmity between them and the Hebrews.

The Dispersion

In 621 BC the Assyrians defeated the northern Hebrew kingdom, Israel, deported its people and replaced them with settlers from deep within the Assyrian empire. The people of Israel were never to return, and although the new settlers adopted the Hebrew religion the people of the southern Hebrew kingdom, Judah, never accepted them.

In time, and with further additions, the newcomers became the Samaritans. The Hebrews refused to allow them to assist with the rebuilding of Jerusalem and the Temple 200 years later, and so set the seal on mutual antagonism between the two peoples.

In any case, from that time onwards, an increasing number of the Hebrew people were living outside Palestine, in great cities such as Babylon, Rome and Alexandria. These Hebrews of the 'dispersion', as they were called, looked to Jerusalem for their religious inspiration and thus retained a sense of national identity, but they were citizens of a wider world than Palestine.

The Land of the Covenant

Thus the Hebrews were able to draw on an enormous range of experience for their religion and for their culture. But the real point is not the range of sources from which the Hebrews obtained their religious materials; rather it is the use that they made of them. They controlled the use of such cultural material by referring it at every point to the experience of the escape from Egypt and the great Covenant which God had made with them during the journey through the wilderness from Egypt to the promised land. The material was adapted and assimilated in ways that brought out the significance of the great Covenant. They borrowed the thoughts and the religious practices of their neighbours, but only so that they could better understand the God who had chosen them and saved them.

For the Hebrews, Palestine was more than a homeland. It was the proof that they had been set apart by God for his own special purposes. Geographically speaking, Palestine is an insignificant and unattractive piece of land, but the Hebrews filled it with significance. In its turn, Palestine played its part in forming the Hebrew character and in providing the Hebrew people with a visible reminder of their identity and purpose. It was the land of the Covenant.

Chapter 2

THE STORY OF THE PEOPLE
OF THE COVENANT

The Old Testament is not just a book about religion. It is also the history of a people, the Hebrew people. Religion, people and history cannot be separated. The people made their discoveries about God through the successes, the failures, the trials and the joys which they experienced in their lives. Their history provides us with the framework for understanding the message they have left us.

The Foundations of Faith

The most important single event in the whole of the Old Testament is the escape from Egypt under the leadership of Moses, about 1250 BC.

The Exodus, as it is called, remained at the very centre of the nation's life. It provided the Hebrew people with the foundations on which they built their faith. It was the central event of their history, to which they returned again and again for guidance and reassurance down through the centuries, even to the present day. The significance of that great event was discussed and explored by the Hebrews whenever they were faced with problems or with changes in fortune. It was their way of thinking out the central truths of their religion and applying them to new circumstances.

Those basic truths never changed, but the people grew in their understanding of them as the Hebrew nation developed. The way they thought about God was closely related to the ways in which Hebrew society developed. Great historical forces, such as conquest or expansion of trade, brought social and political changes to the Hebrew people. Their religion was durable and flexible in the midst of all the changes, and they learned to appreciate its richness.

The First Hebrews

The first Hebrews were wandering shepherd people who led their flocks over vast stretches of land in their search for pasture. Under the leadership of Abraham, Isaac and Jacob they journeyed from the depths of Mesopotamia to the borders of Egypt. There was no real competition between them and the farmers, for their sheep could survive on the sparse vegetation along the borders of the deserts, and they never settled long in one place.

God was a shepherd to them, who led them and protected them at such dangerous times as lambing or moving camp. Because their social life was based on the family, and on the tribe as a collection of closely related families, they also thought of God as a father. They looked to God with the natural loyalty, obedience and affection that members of a family feel towards their head. Their main way of expressing their relationship with God was through the sacrifice of a lamb. The life of a young lamb was fresh from God, so its blood symbolized God's protective power, and to eat such a lamb was to share in God's hospitality.

They took their relationship with God for granted, and sometimes spoke to him with startling familiarity. Almost certainly, they also took it for granted that other tribes, other families, would have other gods.

Little changed, it seems, in their way of life when famine drove them to settle on the borders of Egypt, where one of their number, Joseph, had risen to high office in the royal court.

The Great Escape and the Covenant

A revolution in Egypt brought to power kings who felt no sympathy for the Hebrews on the Egyptian frontier. Their comfortable independence changed dramatically as they were pressed into forced labour and their numbers were controlled. The God of the Hebrews seemed unable to help his oppressed people.

The situation required a leader who could inspire the people to trust God's power. Such a man was found in Moses (see chapter 6: 'Moses, Architect of the Nation'). He confronted the Egyptian king in all his might. He led the people in their escape. He interpreted God to them, and spoke to God on their behalf, when God made his Covenant with them in the desert. Above all, he showed the Hebrew people what the real issue was. It was about the power of God.

When the Hebrews escaped from the mighty power of Egypt, and saw a detachment of the Egyptian army drown in the marshes and treacherous channels of the Sea of Reeds, they realized for the first time that their God was not just another god amongst gods. He was the supreme God. To their amazement, their ancestral God, the God of Abraham, Isaac and Jacob, proved that he was stronger than any of the divine powers on which the Egyptians called. When God now made them his people, and forged an eternal Covenant with them, this meant that he would protect them against the enmity of any other nation on earth.

Later they would realize that such great privileges carried with them equally great responsibilities. They were to be God's ambassadors, called by God to take the message of his love out into all the world, and to guard it faithfully down the centuries. But the full realization of such a vocation lay far in the future. Their immediate task was to consolidate their new Covenant with God, and to change from a loose federation of tribes into a nation.

The Promised Land

Their national base was to be Palestine, or Canaan, as it was then called, where their ancestors had already travelled for so long with their flocks.

The Hebrew struggle to control Canaan was more than a war with the people who already occupied the land. It involved a whole change in the Hebrew way of life. Although they gained the supremacy, they had much to learn from the Canaanites about agriculture and about the organization of life in towns and villages.

There was also the temptation to water down the Hebrew religion by worshipping Canaanite gods, and this temptation recurred in one way or another all through the Old Testament period. But the memory of the great escape, and of the Covenant God had made with them, kept the Hebrew people faithful, and their victories over the Canaanites reassured them about the power of God.

Not long after the Hebrews gained possession of Canaan a new danger threatened their very existence. Invaders from the west established themselves on the Mediterranean coast of Canaan, and forced the Hebrews into submission. The Philistines, as the new rulers were called, were so successful that the very name 'Palestine' comes from them.

The Hebrews realized that the old tribal organization was too divided and too localized to give the people the security they needed. There must be a permanent, central authority to organize defence and give the people unity. As a result, the Hebrews elected a king to rule over them. At first their hopes were dashed, for King Saul and his son Jonathan died in battle against the Philistines. But under the brilliant leadership of David the Philistines were defeated, and the loose federation of Hebrew tribes became a kingdom.

This new form of political authority affected the way in which the Hebrews thought of God. The Covenant was now guarded by the king. But God was their real king, who made his will known to his people through the nation's laws, and ruled them with an authority far greater than any mere head of a family could have. It was God's power which made the king victorious, so he must rule his people and protect them as God's agent.

Kings and Prophets

It was at this time that Jerusalem sprang into prominence as the national capital (see chapter 7: 'Jerusalem'). The great Temple built by David's son, Solomon, provided a central focus for the nation's religious life, and began to replace the old local sanctuaries in importance. Such a religious centre would be needed if the Hebrew people were to retain their sense of national identity. For the new nation split into two kingdoms at Solomon's death, and great international powers began to control Palestine. Hardly ever again would the Hebrew people enjoy political independence.

Even greater was the danger that wealth, and the attractions of other people's gods, would encourage the people to forget their own God and his wonderful Covenant with them. Even the kings themselves betrayed their responsibilities as God's agents.

For five hundred years, a series of great teachers, the prophets, risked their lives to remind the people of their religious inheritance. Not even the kings, royal ministers and priests were safe from their denunciations. Above all, the prophets sprang to the defence of the poor and the weak when the privileged classes oppressed them or treated them with contempt. Elijah and Elisha were the first of these outstanding men during the earlier years of the kingdom, but they were followed by Amos, Hosea, Micah and Isaiah. Hosea led his people to a deeper understanding of God's love through the failure of his own marriage. Isaiah tried in vain to prevent the king from entering into a disastrous alliance with the Assyrians.

During these years, the northern Hebrew kingdom was destroyed by the Assyrians and its people marched off to oblivion. Only Jerusalem remained, and the minority of the Hebrew people who lived in the south, as the whole of Palestine fell under Assyrian rule. A hundred years later, Jeremiah helped reform the nation during a brief period of political freedom, but it soon became clear that only deep misfortune could teach the people their real need for God.

Exile and Rebirth

The Hebrew kingdom had drifted into failure and corruption, until it seemed no better than any other small country of the time. History had shown that there was nothing automatic about the Covenant with God. The people must respond with their whole hearts for God's love to be effective.

In 587 BC the Babylonians destroyed Jerusalem and drove its people into exile. Such prophets as Jeremiah and Ezekiel taught that this was far from being a disaster. If the nation profited from its sufferings, it would return with a new Covenant and renewed dedication to God. Much of the Old Testament as we now know it was shaped by those Hebrews who went into exile in Babylon and by the ones who returned fifty years later to rebuild Jerusalem and create a new people of God. They gathered together all the nation's traditions and laws. They preserved the writings and teachings of the prophets. They showed how the whole sweep of Hebrew history, from the very creation of the world, revealed the majesty and love of God. They collected the literature of their people, from court records to the hymns they sang in the Temple, and from passionate love poems to philosophical writings, and made them the inspiration of a nation.

The Hebrew people could now see the Covenant with God as the key to all that had happened to them, and they could at last understand what God wanted of them. The vague hopes with which the nation had begun its long journey had turned into clear and lasting convictions. Such a history, in which an ancient people learned so much about God, can be a model for any nation's history. Through it all there shines an impressive honesty, so that even the nation's mistakes become lessons for others.

But above all, the Hebrew people, whose history this is, share with us all that they learned about God and his Covenant. In the pages of the Old Testament, they show how their Covenant with God can become God's Covenant with the whole world, not merely with the Hebrew nation.

Chapter 3

EVERYDAY LIFE

The Old Testament is a book about God, but everything it tells us about God comes to us through people seen in their families, their neighbourhoods and their jobs.

Once we have made allowances for the differences of time and the part of the world where the Hebrew people lived, their lives were very similar to our own. The things that really matter, such as home life, conditions of work and security, are just the things which concern us too. The wonderful discoveries they made about God were all influenced by their personal lives. It was because God meant so much to them in everyday matters that their discoveries are so interesting to people at all times and in all places.

The Family

In the very early days, before the Hebrews settled down in Canaan, they lived as shepherds, always moving their flocks of sheep to new pastures. Their black-tented camps were never in one place for very long. Under these circumstances, the family was the most important unit of all, and the father of the family wielded absolute authority over his wife, his children and the people who shared the camp. Every family unit strove to be self-sufficient, like the early pioneers of the United States or the isolated towns of medieval Europe. The head of the family made the decisions about marriage, work and the whole economic life of the community. His word was law, and he made the law of the family as problems arose and decisions had to be made. In legal terms, this was 'case law', built from precedents and the new situations of each recurring day.

But they were not isolated decisions, nor was it a tyrannical authority. Because the family was the social unit, every member of the community was able to make his or her opinion known. The very way of life made for open government, for everyone in the camp knew everything that was going on.

Such a social situation had a profound effect on the way the Hebrews thought about God. Above all, he was a father to them, whom they could obey with confidence. He shared their lives and their concerns. He knew their needs.

Marriage

In the very early days, it seems that monogamy was the norm amongst the Hebrew people : one husband married one wife. Only if the wife proved barren did the husband take a second partner, and that only with the full approval of his official wife, to provide him with an heir. Any other partners were inferior, and counted as little more than slaves.

Later, the custom grew of allowing a man to take a number of wives. Even so, he had to be able to support them, and there must have been few who could afford the luxury, and problems, of such an extended family group. In any case, marriage involved a financial outlay on the husband's part, for he had to make a payment to the father of his bride, and sometimes he provided the bride herself with a dowry. Such customs arose from the economic value of any person at a time when everyone helped support the family unit. On marriage, the wife left her own family and joined that of her husband, so her labour was lost to her own people.

There is no firm evidence about the minimum age for marriage, but it may have been as young as twelve years. In any case, a period of engagement was normal, during which time some kind of joint responsibility was legally recognized. When property and family alliances were so important, it is not surprising that marriages were 'arranged' by the parents, or at least by negotiations between the husband and the bride's father.

The key moment in the marriage ceremony came when the bride, in all her finery, jewels and veil, entered her husband's tent or house. He had gone on ahead of her with his friends and, perhaps, musicians. The bride thus entered her husband's family symbolically and literally, and the feasting would go on for a full seven days. The marriage was consummated on the first night, and the bride kept proof that she had been a virgin at the time of her marriage. Such evidence could be important if her husband decided to divorce her. Divorce was all too easy for the husband, though not for the wife. He only had to pronounce, before witnesses, that she was no longer his wife nor he her husband. But there were some restrictions on divorce, and one of them was a false accusation by the husband that his wife had not been a virgin at the time of marriage.

The Hebrews drew a sharp distinction between adultery – sexual intercourse with another's wife – and fornication. The latter was no more a crime than was prostitution, but adultery carried the death penalty because it violated another person's rights.

One further aspect of marriage shows how important it was to secure an heir. If a man died before his wife had borne him a son, his brother had to take the wife, to keep the first husband's name alive by procuring an heir for him. Few Hebrews believed in immortality or resurrection, and a man lived on only in his sons.

Children

Children were cherished and loved in the Hebrew family. Indeed, they were the true sign of blessedness, and the man or woman who died childless was counted most unfortunate. Sons were prized above daughters, because of the protection and strength they promised, and the eldest son had privileges above his brothers. But there was no clear custom of the eldest always inheriting responsibility and leadership. Such positions were too important to leave to chance of birth, so they depended rather on the father's choice amongst his sons.

The name given to a child always had a special significance. Sometimes it reflected the hopes of the parents, or it referred to a special event associated with the child's birth. For all that the father was so important, it was the mother who gave her child its name.

On the eighth day after birth, a boy underwent circumcision, in which his father cut away the foreskin of the boy's penis. Originally, this rite was performed at puberty, to show that the boy was now of marriageable age and ready to take his place as an adult member of the community. Later, it acquired religious significance, and showed that the child now shared in the Covenant with God, which had created the Hebrew nation. Naturally, parents wanted this privilege for their sons as soon as possible, so the operation was performed on the baby child.

The mother was responsible for the early education of her children, and for the whole education of daughters. Father soon took over responsibility for the education of sons in the nation's religion and the traditions. Formal schools do not seem to have been established until the very end of the Old Testament period, but from the earliest times priests and prophets both had teaching responsibilities. This was for the instruction and guidance of adults, as much as children, and was particularly associated with the religious sanctuaries.

In 622 BC the local sanctuaries were suppressed in favour of the Temple in Jerusalem, and this centralization was strengthened by the fifty years of exile in Babylon shortly afterwards. The synagogues, or local meeting houses, probably developed as a result, each with its 'rabbi' or teacher. But the main responsibility for education remained with the father.

Professions and Trades

When the future was always so uncertain, even the sons of
the wealthy were taught a trade by which they could earn
a living if they fell on hard times. Fathers taught their
sons their own trades, and in the case of the priesthood,
the profession was strictly hereditary. In the larger towns,
craftsmen of the same craft all worked in the same street,
which took its name from them. In the country, there
were sometimes specialist villages famed for particular
skills, much as a modern town may be known for its
weaving or engineering.

Before the time of King David, there were few social
distinctions, apart from the natural power and honour
belonging to the heads of families. As the kings, from
David onwards, established a strong central government,
a new class of royal officials developed with special privileges. These were the officers of the new standing army,
governors of the various districts into which the country
was divided, and officials responsible for the collection
of taxes or the administration of justice.

Sharp differences in wealth began to show. Towns and
villages had once been composed of houses which were all
of much the same size. Soon there were conspicuously
large houses in some districts and small hovels in other
parts. Speculation, trade and land grants from the king
all helped to create a wealthy stratum in Hebrew society,
and a corresponding group of the deprived and under-
privileged. Such prophets as Amos, Hosea and Isaiah denounced the social injustice of their times. People without
either land of their own or a skilled trade, could sell their
labour for a daily wage. The poor and destitute depended
on grain and fruit left behind in the fields when the harvest
was collected.

Slavery

Slavery was a universal fact of the ancient world, and a
threat hanging over everyone's head. Defeat in war meant

slavery for whole populations, as did debt. The slave was simply the property of his or her owner.

The Hebrews drew a distinction between slaves of their own nation, and foreign slaves. Foreigners could be acquired by capture or purchase. The law of the 'sabbath' or seventh-day rest applied equally to slaves, but apart from this they had no rights. For Hebrews themselves there were a whole range of protective laws, even when they were slaves. They must be offered their freedom after six years, and given sufficient in money or goods to give them a start in life again. Only if they refused such freedom were Hebrews enslaved for life. Before a Hebrew could be enslaved for debt, his or her male relatives must try to redeem the situation with money or property. Freedom was a family responsibility.

The Law

The many different legal terms in use in the Old Testament show the many ways in which Hebrew law developed; but whatever the origins of the various laws, they all derived their authority from God. Above all, God was the source of law, and of the order which law expressed.

The divine origins of the law are shown most dramatically through the casting of lots to obtain decisions. The priests were responsible for obtaining this form of judgement, and the whole idea of law in general was derived from it. God revealed his will through the priests, and such decisions were thus law. The great historical events in the nation's history, such as the escape from Egypt, confirmed these revelations by God in response to his people's questions.

In everyday life, most people would come into contact with law through the cases decided by the head of the family or by the village elders in public. Such cases were decided by precedent and common sense, with modification of past decisions when the circumstances differed. *Commandments* and *statutes* were laws made by an authority such as the king, and promulgated in writing. There was a different form of words for such edicts. But whatever the sources of the various laws, they had two things in common. They were always referred back to God for their ultimate authority, and they applied equally to every member of the community, whatever his or her status might be.

That God is the ultimate source of all law is shown vividly by the position given to the legal codes in the Old Testament. No matter when a particular law first emerged, they were all put into the mouth of Moses, during the journey through the wilderness after the escape from Egypt and the great Covenant with God. Thus all Hebrew law will be found in the Books of Exodus, Leviticus, Numbers or Deuteronomy.

Again, the escape from Egypt placed God's value on every member of the Hebrew community, for there was no selection process on grounds of birth, class, wealth, education or any other basis. Therefore there could be no such distinctions before the law. This principle was established clearly when King David himself was brought to book by the prophet Nathan. Whatever might happen in practice as fallible and weak human beings administered the law, in theory the law was absolutely impartial.

Just as law protected the community of God's people, so the whole community took part in any punishment to be meted out. Execution was normally by stoning. The witnesses whose evidence had been decisive were made responsible for starting the execution, and every member of the community was expected to share in the killing of the guilty criminal. There was true community of responsibility.

Religion

Everyday life was so permeated by religion that it is misleading to think of it as something distinct. Every uncertainty of life, and every special occasion, had its religious significance. Moreover, the ordinary routine of life was marked by a systematic cycle of feasts, so that God was acknowledged as the normal background to all activity.

The weekly sabbath day's rest had a double significance, both as a reminder of the creation itself, continuously sustained by God's almighty power, and as a commemoration of the escape from Egypt, when God showed his special concern for the Hebrew people. Such worship took place within the family.

Passover, the spring feast, was also located within the family. Whatever its origins, it became indelibly associated with the escape from Egypt, and all other annual feasts took their meaning from the Passover. At Passover, the family gathered to sacrifice a lamb, and re-enact the haste of the night of escape. In vivid imagination, everyone returned to Egypt on that night, and renewed their gratitude to God for their liberty and their land. The three main harvest festivals then took their significance from the Passover. In the harvest, God extended his saving love and provided his people with the means of life.

For the first six centuries of their time in Palestine, the people used local sanctuaries for their worship. Each local shrine would have its special associations with the history of the district and with the families who lived near to it. The sanctuary priests told the old, familiar stories to the worshippers as they gathered for the harvest festivals. Later it was decreed that sacrifices were permitted only in Jerusalem, and the great Temple became a centre of pilgrimage for the whole country. For Hebrews in outlying parts, or in foreign countries, the pilgrimage to Jerusalem would add another dimension to their religious experience, just as it does for so many people today.

For the rich, from the king downwards, sacrifices were lavish occasions with many valuable oxen as the victims. But the laws governing worship made it possible for the poor to offer merely a pigeon or a handful of meal. In any case, the sacrifices were public occasions, and anyone could feel that he or she was sharing in the offering as a Hebrew chosen by God. Nowhere is this sense of religious solidarity shown more clearly than in the psalms. These poems and hymns expressed the feelings of the congregation as they worshipped, and were their main way of taking part in the vividly colourful ceremonies.

The priesthood grew in importance and power down the centuries, until it replaced the kings themselves as the highest authority. But the priests were not remote from the people. Even when they could only perform their main functions in the Temple in Jerusalem, the priests lived throughout the country and only travelled to the capital city when their turn of office fell due.

Town and Country

In one sense, all life in Old Testament times was rural, for there were no conurbations in Palestine as there are today, or as Rome or Alexandria became in the ancient world. Even the inhabitants of Jerusalem or Samaria knew that they depended on the crops which grew near their city walls, and everywhere else 'cities' were no more than fortified settlements from which the people farmed their land. Most towns had, at most, six or seven hundred inhabitants, who would each of them be able to know everyone else's business. There could be little privacy in the tight huddle of houses in an ancient city. Immediately inside the only gate lay the market place. It was a place for news and gossip, as travellers arrived. It was also the place where legal cases were heard and decided. The inhabitants needed no other means of communication or information.

But there was a real difference in feeling between the capital, Jerusalem, and the rest of the country. Jerusalem was a new city, so far as the Hebrews were concerned, dating only from King David's reign when he made it his capital. As such, it represented all the new ideas about centralized government, and the nation as the main object of loyalty. By contrast, the country districts were the seats of loyalty to the family and the old way of life represented by patriarchs like Abraham, Isaac and Jacob. For such people, the family was the real centre of authority. Many of the prophets who so strongly denounced luxury and injustice were country-born. They looked back to the old Covenant given to the people through Moses, and the old ways of worship, rather than to the new meaning placed on the Covenant by David and the court prophets. But the Hebrew religion was strong enough to overcome such differences, and very few of these tensions show in the Old Testament.

In all, the whole country could not have had more than a million inhabitants at any stage in its history. Even more significantly, it was small enough for all the people to share equally in such national disasters as famine, plague or foreign invasion. At such times they were united by their common misfortune, whatever differences local conditions or family history might make.

Chapter 4

THROUGH JEWISH EYES

If you want to understand Shakespeare's plays really well, you need to look at life through the eyes of an Englishman living in the 1600s. Similarly, if a person wants to read the Bible with understanding, he needs ideally to be familiar with the mentality and outlook of a Jew living in the Palestine of 2000-3000 years ago. Now this is not easy. It's not easy to shed the approach to life of a westerner living in the technological world of the twentieth century and attempt instead to see things through the eyes of a Jew living in a world very different from our own.

Pre-Scientific
We call this world 'Pre-scientific'. Science has made twentieth-century men familiar with the causes of weather changes, of thunder and lightning, of eclipses. We know that our earth is a tiny speck in a limitless universe, that our sun is but one of a thousand million suns in our galaxy alone, and that there are at the very least a hundred million other galaxies similar to our own. There is hardly a fact of nature we cannot explain rationally.

The Jew of Bible times knew nothing of these things. For him, the earth was the centre of the universe. Certainly he admired as God's great handiwork the stars shining in the night sky, but he had absolutely no conception of the vastness of space. Heaven, God's throne, was 'above': the flat earth on which man dwelt was supported by pillars over Hades – the underworld. It is true that the authors of the creation stories in Genesis, chapters 1 and 2, are not attempting to give scientific accounts of the origins of our world, but the descriptions of creation given there do show something of the very primitive outlook of this nomadic people, an outlook on the world of nature (definitely *not* the world of people, of which they had a sophisticated understanding) not unlike that of a five-year-old child of today.

Respecter of Persons

We believe that the authors and editors of the Bible books – we say 'authors and editors' because some of the books were first spoken and memorized before, many years later, being edited into written form – were inspired by God. Although the whole subject of inspiration is beyond the scope of the present work, nevertheless, put perhaps somewhat over-simply, it could be understood as meaning that the *general sense* conveyed by the writers was the sense intended by God, the Inspirer. Inspiration does not mean that the Bible authors were God's secretaries, and that God dictated to them exactly what they had to write down. God respects people: he doesn't use them. And so too God accepted the Bible authors as they were, with the character and outlook they possessed.

God did not try to inject into them a scientific understanding that would belong to a later age. He simply helped them to reflect upon and see in their experiences the ways of God with men, and having reflected, to put their thoughts into a form that would be available for posterity.

A Tragic Marriage

Let's look at an example: one of the prophets, Hosea (see page 190) made a disastrous marriage. His wife, Gomer, deserted him and eventually became a prostitute. Despite the humiliation of it all, he forgave her and took her back into his home. But that was not all; Hosea saw in this personal experience something of God's unconditional love and forgiveness even when his people were faithless and strayed 'after false gods'. Hosea was inspired to write of the understanding of God's mercy and compassion that he had glimpsed through the tears he had shed at his own personal tragedy.

So it was with all the authors of the Bible books: they reflected on their diverse experiences and saw in them the hand of God. God's inspiration did not stop them from being men truly of their time. Therefore if we are to grasp the sense of the message God today reveals to us through them, we must move back in time and try to see things through their eyes.

Perhaps the point of difference most difficult for the twentieth-century westerner to grasp is the Biblical Jews' understanding of history, and the way they recorded it. We insist on accuracy and detail. For example, a recent book about World War II gives a multiplicity of verifiable details – about the weather, actual conversations, clothing, feelings, ages, backgrounds – for a group of men taking part in an assault on a bridge. The author even relates the brand of beer the captain drank during a lull in the battle!

Is it True?

Jews were indifferent to such a manner of recording events. It is noticeable for example, that although the Bible is largely about people, there is hardly one description of a particular person. We have no description of even Jesus's physical appearance. The questions we frequently ask when we see a TV documentary, or read a story: 'Was it true?' 'Did it really happen?' – those questions would never have occurred to the Jewish readers of the holy books.

They were very careless of historical accuracy. If they wanted to say that a man was very old before he died, they would write 'His life lasted two hundred and five years; then he died' (see, for example, Genesis 11:32). In Exodus 12:41 the number of people who escaped from Egypt is given as 'Six hundred thousand on the march – all men – not counting their families'. This is quite an impossible number; if it is taken as literally exact, a million people must have been journeying across the desert. And for forty years? Here again we have to take care to think after the manner of the Bible writers.

Certain numbers had a consistent significance. For example, forty is usually associated with a time of preparation – forty years in the desert before arrival at the promised land, forty days' fast in the desert before Jesus announced the coming of the Kingdom, forty days from the Resurrection to the coming of the Spirit at Pentecost. Twelve usually indicated a universality of peoples, 'the twelve tribes'. Seven and three indicated perfection, (and so six, being neither seven nor three, indicated something imperfect – thus the number of the Beast in Revelation is given as 6666, about as bad as could be). Four indicated a geographical universality – 'the four corners of the earth'.

It shouldn't be thought that there is little of historical fact in the Bible. There is plenty. But the Jews were interested in historical facts only in so far as those historical facts revealed the readiness of God to save his people. The question the Jew asked after reading, for example, the two accounts of the Red Sea crossing (each of which explains differently how it was achieved), was not 'Which of these accounts describes what really happened?' It would never have occurred to him to ask that question. The question he would ask would rather have been 'What truth do these accounts tell me about God and his people?' And it is the question we must ask too.

Chapter 5

A CHILD'S VISION OF LIFE

Not for the child the world of concepts and abstract thoughts. The child thinks mainly in pictures. So too with the Jew of Bible times. He didn't attempt to define God. Our so-called definitions of God, 'Supreme Being', 'Ultimate Reality', 'the Ground of our Being', 'the Absolute' – all these abstract concepts would have been barely intelligible to the Jew. He painted pictures of God in words.

As a mother:

As a mother comforts her child,
will I comfort you. (Isaiah 66 : 13)

As an eagle:

Like an eagle teaching its young to fly,
catching them safely on its spreading wings. (Deuteronomy 32 : 11)

As a rock:

He is the rock, his work is perfect. (Deuteronomy 32 : 4)

As a father:

As kind as a father is to his children
so kind is the Lord to those who honour him. (Psalm 103 : 13)

I picked them up and held them to
my cheek
I bent down to them and fed them. (Hosea 11 : 4)

As a lover:

I will love them with all my heart
for my anger has turned from them. (Hosea 14 : 4)

The Bible is full of magnificent word pictures, and in this sense it is much easier to read than many a present-day theological work. True, some of the pictures (as also our dreams) are hard to interpret. But the key to a right understanding is to be sure we know in what particular 'literary form' the book we are reading is cast. When we pick up a book of poems we judge its contents as poetry not as prose. 'My love is like a red red rose' is a poetic statement, not a horticultural one taken from a gardening magazine. If we are reading a parable such as the Good Samaritan (and some of the books of the Old Testament are parables rather than history), we don't ask, 'What was the cost of bed and breakfast at the inn?'

An Evening's Television
A look at this evening's programmes on TV and radio will illustrate this point. It is very likely that it will contain a number of literary forms: short story, drama, documentary about the past, poetry, cartoon, song, news. We don't get worked up if the principal character in a soap opera is taken to hospital; we accept it as part of the drama and telling us some sort of truth. However, we are very upset if the newscaster tells us there has been a bad train crash. We have used our critical faculty to discriminate between the two 'literary forms'. Similarly, one of the Bible books may purport to give many historical facts (as for example in Maccabees), another may be a short story (the Book of Judith), another may be poetry (the Song of Songs), another may be legend (the story of Samson).

There are many other 'literary forms' in the Bible – in fact some of the books of the Bible contain several forms, and the question we need to ask ourselves as we begin to read is this: 'What form of literature am I reading?' If I haven't got a clear answer, I am likely to misunderstand it.

Everything to God
A child refers everything to his parents. If he is given a toy, he will take it straight away to show them. Similarly if he is hurt, he will run first of all to his mother and father. A little boy fell off his bike in the road where I live; he cut himself quite badly, but he ran off without crying, leaving

his bike where it lay. I said to the child who had been playing with him – 'He's a brave boy. Not a tear'. She replied, 'He runs home and then he cries to his mother'.

So it was with the Jews, they referred everything to God, good and bad, fears and hopes. They ignored what we would call 'secondary causes'. If there is a plague of flies, we attribute it to the peculiar weather conditions and prevailing wind. The Jews simply ignored such secondary causes: they would say quite simply, 'God sent the plague . . .' If a priest were to die suddenly during a ceremony, we might say, 'He was struck down by a coronary thrombosis'. The Jews would have said – 'God struck him down'. 'Uzzah stretched his hand out to the ark of God and steadied it as the oxen were making it tilt . . . and God struck him down on the spot.' (2 Samuel 6 : 6)

Family Comes First

The Jew of Bible times was not at all child-like in his sense of community. Most young children are very self-centred and individualistic, their horizons are foreshortened. In contrast, the Jew's feeling of loyalty to the community far outweighed his individualistic tendencies. Almost everything was seen in the light of the community – 'Will this harm or help the great family to which I belong?' The Jew hardly thought of God as being interested in himself as an individual. It was God's care for his people that preoccupied him.

As we shall see, nearly all the books of the Old Testament were written without any expectation of a life after death – no reward, no punishment – at the most, just the merest wraith-like semi-existence in a shadowy Hades –

The living know at least that they will die,

the dead know nothing; no more reward for them,

their memory has passed out of mind. (Ecclesiastes 8 : 5)

Small wonder then that this people sought a continued existence, if not individually then at least in their community.

Chapter 6

MOSES, ARCHITECT OF
THE NATION

Moses towers over the other characters in the Old Testament like a colossus.

He grew up amidst the luxury of the Egyptian royal court. As a young man he fled to the loneliness and privation of the desert, and there he spoke with God. He confronted all the might of Egypt, in the person of the Pharaoh, its divine king. He led his people out into the desert and across the marshes and channels at the end of the Red Sea, when many of them must have feared that he was taking them to their deaths. He mediated between his people and God at the sacred mountain, when God made his Covenant with them and turned them into a chosen nation. He guided the new nation through the wilderness and left it with a blueprint for the new kind of life it must lead when it finally took possession of Canaan. He stands out from the pages of the Old Testament as God's master workman, who forged a mighty new tool for God and his world. Moses made the Hebrew people from the raw materials that God gave to him.

Information

At first sight the amount of information available about Moses is vast. Four of the Bible's largest books, Exodus, Leviticus, Numbers and Deuteronomy, are entirely devoted to him. They tell us about his life, his teaching, his simple-minded devotion to God, and the part he played in the creation of the Hebrew nation. There is more information about Moses than we have about any other Biblical character, including Jesus himself. The Moses passages in those four books near the beginning of the Old Testament occupy nearly twice as much space as the gospels occupy in the New Testament.

But as soon as we have said this the obvious objection stands out. In the form in which we now have it, most of this material about Moses belongs to later periods of Hebrew history. The stories about Moses describe the times when the Hebrews were enslaved in Egypt, and Moses led them out to start a new life in the promised land. But some of this information was not written down until as much as seven centuries later. At first sight this may seem to make the material of little use to us, but in fact it clears the way for another approach, which is more valuable and relevant to us than one which takes the Bible literally in every detail.

A Special Purpose

Later generations of Hebrews re-wrote and expanded the stories about Moses for their own times, and they did so for a special purpose. They needed the religion given to them by Moses, but they needed it in a form which made sense of their own problems and their new situations. The message Moses gave had to be up-dated if it was to meet their needs without losing any of the truth which gave it such impressive power.

The world of the Hebrews was no more a static one than is our own. The people were exposed to constant pressures and challenges from the neighbouring peoples, from the great powers which occupied their country for almost all of their history, and from the economic changes through which they passed. The Hebrews responded to all these pressures successfully, and adapted themselves to the new situations. The beliefs passed down from Moses were their life-line, so that they never lost their faith in the living presence and power of God, nor their confidence in their national vocation. The traditions passed down from Moses gave them a stable pattern in the midst of all the forces of change.

King David

The first great change in their way of life, with all the strains that went with it, came at the time of King David. David defeated the nation's enemies and gave it security, and he then led his people through a great economic change, a change as great as the technological revolution which is still at work in our own times. The bulk of the Hebrew people turned from the life of wandering shepherds and became settled farmers, with towns and villages and a central government in Jerusalem.

If the religion of Moses had continued only to be the faith of shepherds, it would have faded away as the nation changed its way of life. David, under the inspiration of the prophet Nathan, adapted the Covenant which God had made with the people through Moses, and made it the foundation of the new national government. From now on the people would be ruled by kings, but they would be kings who ruled in the spirit of Moses. The kings would be the ministers of God's Covenant.

To symbolize this vital truth, King David brought the sacred Ark of the Covenant to Jerusalem. In this box were the tablets of stone on which the Ten Commandments had been carved, which Moses had brought to the people from God. Moses's vision of the eternal relationship of the Hebrew nation to God was now enshrined at the heart of the nation's new capital by King David. It is as if the journey through the wilderness to the promised land had at last ended at Jerusalem.

Worship

In a similar way the nation's worship was adapted to meet the needs of the new economic patterns. The old Hebrew religion had been a shepherd's religion, and the main feast a shepherd's feast. This was the Passover when each family ate a lamb in a sacred meal with God, and smeared the lamb's blood on the door posts of their houses to gain divine protection from any evil which might threaten them.

The people were now farmers, and a series of great harvest festivals was added to the shepherd feast of the Passover. The Passover was not enough. Even the Temple in Jerusalem and the Ark of the Covenant were not enough. The people's needs must be met by relevant worship, expressed in forms which made immediate impact on them. The new harvest festivals showed the people that the God of Moses was also the God of the harvest. Their God, the God who had brought their ancestors out of Egypt, was showing his power and his love for them in the crops that they grew in their fields.

Law

That same love was brought to bear on every intimate detail of the people's lives through the law. Under Moses the people had learned that the law set out the pattern of their new lives as God's chosen people. It taught them how they must treat each other if they were to be faithful to the God who had saved them, and who was now using them to show his goodness and his love to all the world.

So all of the nation's laws, right down through its history, were put into the mouth of Moses. This is a strange thing to do, but it conveys a fundamental truth. As the laws grew and developed to meet new situations and changing needs, they remained faithful to the insights which Moses had first given to his people. Legislators of future generations asked themselves what Moses would have decided if he had been in their place, and so the whole body of the nation's law became an expression of the religion of Moses.

Inspiration

Finally, and above all, at the moment of supreme need the nation's leaders looked back to Moses for inspiration, so that their people could undertake a task greater than any that the nation had faced before.

Their task was no less than to return to the ruins of Jerusalem, and their deserted land, after fifty years of exile, and to build the nation anew. It was then that the nation's religious leaders gathered together all the stories and traditions of Moses, all the developments in law and worship, and stitched them together in one mighty and continuous story. It is this picture of Moses which we have inherited in the opening books of the Old Testament.

It is a testimony to the wonderful work of those ancient story-tellers that those books about Moses are as inspiring and moving to people today as they were to the people for whom they were originally written. Whenever people have been enslaved or oppressed, they have found hope and encouragement in Moses's unswerving testimony to the God of righteousness and love. He saved the Hebrew people in their helplessness and misery, and made them a nation of priests, a royal and proud people destined to carry his name down the centuries and across the world. People will willingly give their lives to a God such as this.

A Dynamic Faith

The further back one goes, peeling off the layers of editing and relating sources to the period when they reached written form, the more meagre the information about Moses becomes. Yet one senses the presence of a towering figure, a personality who set his mark indelibly on the nation and stamped it with the pattern of his own faith.

It is a dynamic faith, which has proved to be infinitely adaptable and applicable down through the centuries. Moses gave the people who followed him a point of view which they could apply to their own new situations, to help them respond to God's love with confidence and devotion. Their new responses developed and expressed beliefs and ideals which united the people with their beginnings and provided them with a sense of identity.

They were the people of God, and they were responding to the presence of God just as their forefathers did.

No one knows for sure exactly where Moses was buried, nor is there any stone monument to him. His monument is the Hebrew people and the beliefs about God which the world has inherited from them.

Chapter 7

JERUSALEM

Few sights can be more breathtaking today than the ancient parts of the city of Jerusalem. Seen from the Mount of Olives in the early morning, bathed in the first rays of the sun, it seems the very symbol of security and peace. Great walls enclose it. Immediately within the walls, on the eastward side, the city is dominated by the enormous stone platform on which the famous Temple once stood. Along its southern flanks, walls tower above the deep valley. On the far side of this sacred site a patchwork of roofs indicates the tightly huddled houses and shops, the winding, covered streets and dark flights of stone steps which form the Old City.

For most people, Jerusalem is inseparably associated with the Hebrew people. Yet it was eight centuries after Abraham's time before the Hebrews gained possession of the city and made it their capital.

King David's City

During those early years, Jerusalem belonged to the Jebusites, a Canaanite people who lived in the rocky region where the central range of hills in Palestine hangs over the edge of the Jordan valley. Their tiny city was perched on a narrow ridge near a spring of water, and its position made it well-nigh impregnable. It was an inconvenient site, for most of the houses had to be built on steep slopes, but in those times, as now, people had to give a high priority to defence against possible enemies. In the course of the centuries Jerusalem has almost abandoned that first rocky ridge, and the city has edged northwards on to flatter ground as people have sought better sites for their houses. But it was the defensive potential of the ancient city's first site which appealed to King David when he chose it to be the capital city of the new Hebrew kingdom.

Above all, Jerusalem is David's city, and the memorial of his achievement. David made Jerusalem a symbol of unity for his scattered and divided people, when he captured it from the Jebusites and moved the sacred Ark of the Covenant into it. The ancient religious traditions of the wandering Hebrew people had found a permanent home as they settled down to farm the country they had wrested from the Canaanites and defended against the Philistines.

The Temple

David's son, Solomon, set the seal on his father's achievement by building the first Temple. Its magnificence took the breath away from the Queen of Sheba, when she visited Solomon, and from then onwards Jerusalem's central importance was sustained by the Temple and the worship associated with it. When Solomon died the kingdom split into two states at war with each other, and Jerusalem remained the capital only of the southern, smaller, kingdom of Judah. But its religious prestige was already greater than its political authority, and in the end the priests of the Temple in Jerusalem became the real rulers of the whole of the Hebrew people.

By modern standards the Temple was a small building, no more than ninety feet long, thirty feet wide and forty-five feet high. In the 'Holy of Holies', the innermost room of the Temple, the Ark of the Covenant was kept in total darkness. No layman ever entered that sacred place, and the temple priests only visited it on rare occasions of the highest religious significance. Most of the Temple's length was occupied by the 'Holy Place', which was separated from the 'Holy of Holies' by double doors. This richly panelled room was illuminated by windows set high in the walls and was approached through a porch flanked by two great bronze pillars.

Out in the open, in front of the pillars, was an enormous square altar fifteen feet high and with sides thirty feet long. In the solemn sacrifices which were the main feature of ancient Hebrew worship, the slaughtered animals were burned on this altar. The worshippers gathered in the courtyards surrounding the Temple within sight of the central building.

Ruined and Rebuilt

As the population of the city grew more ground was enclosed by defensive walls. On more than one occasion those walls defeated the efforts of great armies to capture the city, including the Assyrians, but the city did twice fall to the Babylonians (in 598 BC and 587 BC), and on the second occasion the conquerors deported its people and reduced city and Temple to rubble.

For fifty years Jerusalem lay in ruins. The returning exiles rebuilt the city, but the rule of the Hebrew kings had finished for ever, and from then onwards the new Hebrew community was led by the temple priests. The new Temple lasted more than five hundred years, until the very end of the Old Testament period, when Herod replaced it with a magnificent new Temple which took ten years to build.

That third Temple survived the shortest time of all, for in AD 70 city and Temple were again destroyed in the bitter war fought between the Jews and the Romans. Herod extended the courtyards on foundations of huge stone blocks, and it is this great platform which survives until today. The most probable site of the Temple itself has been occupied for the last thirteen hundred years by a very beautiful Moslem shrine, 'The Dome of the Rock'.

Although it is best known as the City of David, Jerusalem means far more than King David and the other famous people associated with it. Rather, it focuses the faith and religious fervour of countless millions of people,

Jews, Christians and Moslems. These are the people who have lived in this city, travelled on pilgrimage to it, or looked to it for inspiration. But it is the people of the Old Testament who first made Jerusalem a symbol of God's presence in his world, and so made it a city for all peoples.

Chapter 8

THE MESSIAH

The word 'Messiah' has rich and moving associations for many people. It awakens memories of Handel's great oratorio. It is sometimes used as the most impressive possible description one can apply to an outstanding leader, who can inspire a whole people in a period of supreme danger. And for Christians it means Jesus.

Just as the word can mean many things nowadays, so too it had many associations in Old Testament times. In fact, there does not seem to have been any simple, coherent belief about the Messiah amongst the ancient Hebrews. Many different strands were woven together, and in different combinations, but all of them were ways of expressing utter confidence in God.

The Messiah was the symbol of God's steadfast faithfulness, his righteousness and his power to overcome all opposition. Deep in their hearts the Hebrews believed that the world was entirely God's world, and that his will would triumph in the end. Yet such a belief was never an abstract, academic one. It had its roots and its power in the everyday events of the people's lives, whether at a family level or at the level of the nation as a whole. The words and images which they used to express this hope were taken from the whole range of their ordinary every-day lives. Taken literally, 'Messiah' means 'anointed'. Hebrew kings and priests had consecrated oils poured on them at their coronation or ordination to show that they had been set apart for God's service and had been given authority and power by God himself. This vivid ceremony then became a natural symbol for the leader whom God would send to save his people and rule them perfectly in God's love.

A New Covenant

When the Hebrews went on to describe the kind of kingdom that the Messiah would create, and the kind of person he would be, they drew on experiences from their own national history. At the centre of that history were the escape from Egypt and the Covenant they made with God at Mount Sinai under the leadership of Moses. This was the moment when God made it unmistakably clear that he was more powerful than any forces which might try to oppose him, and that he used that power to save his people from everything which endangered their liberty, their peace or their prosperity. The Covenant guaranteed God's active power amongst them and expressed the people's own response to God's saving presence. This is why the relationship became one of love.

So when the people began to look forward to a new kingdom ruled by God's Messiah, they thought of a new Covenant, which would be so attractive and so effective that everyone would live happily within it. This is why so many of the Messianic passages in the prophets' writings use the idea of a journey in which God leads his people into a new life.

A Perfect King

Although the Exodus and the Covenant provided the essential background without which there could be no Messianic hope, the other strong image in the minds of the people was the idea of kingship, and particularly the kingship of David.

In fact this idea was so strong that the hope for a Messiah first blossomed when David's successors proved to be such bad kings. As the people became disillusioned with their kings, they felt that God would undo the disasters which the kings had brought upon them. God would send them a perfect king, filled with the divine power, who would have none of the weaknesses which mere human kings had shown. The Messiah would be a

son of David, because David was the best model that the
people had for a successful ruler, but he would succeed
where David's sons, and indeed David himself, had so
often failed.

Land, City and Temple

Other obvious symbols were Palestine itself, Jerusalem
and the Temple. The Covenant was always associated
with the promised land. And so the Messiah would rule
over the territory which would be the sanctuary for the
Hebrew people and the centre for the Messiah's world-
wide rule. It would also be a place of secure prosperity,
a land 'flowing in milk and honey' where famine and
privation would never be known again. Naturally enough,
Jerusalem and the Temple were to be the centre of the
Messiah's holy land. From the time of Solomon, when the
first Temple was built to house the Ark of the Covenant,
until the Jewish war more than a thousand years later
when the Temple was finally destroyed during the Roman
siege of Jerusalem, this sacred complex of buildings and
courtyards had been the guarantee of God's presence
amongst his people.

From 622 BC onwards the Temple in Jerusalem was
the only place in the whole world where the Hebrews
could offer sacrifice to God, and so bring the full power
of the Covenant to bear on their everyday lives. It was
the centre of pilgrimage to which Hebrews came from all
over the world, so it was obvious that in the Messianic
age all nations would flock as pilgrims to Jerusalem's
Temple to seek God.

Lesser Images

Round these central ideas about the Messiah and his
kingdom there were a host of lesser images, some of them
of great poetic power.

First there was the idea of the 'remnant', which would
always survive no matter how efficiently the Hebrews'

enemies tried to stamp them out. This remnant would be the nucleus of the new Messianic nation. Then there was the beautiful image of the bride and the bridegroom, in which the Hebrews saw their nation as the bride of God, and mother of a Messianic family which would extend throughout the world. With memories of their early history, the Hebrews saw the Messiah as the shepherd who would fight for his sheep, recapture them from the people who had stolen them, and protect them against all their enemies.

But one of the strangest and most vivid of the images is the title 'son of man' in the prophet Daniel. There the armies of the saints would come on the clouds of heaven led by a man on whom God had conferred supreme authority. After the final great battle this son of man would rule over God's eternal Messianic empire.

Suffering

Only once does the Old Testament suggest that God's purpose might involve some kind of personal suffering by a national leader. Towards the end of the Book of the Prophet Isaiah (in passages written by an anonymous prophet who lived 200 years later than Isaiah himself) there are four poems about a servant of God who would suffer because of his determination to remain faithful to God. This servant allows nothing to compromise his righteousness and his determination to bring the knowledge of God to all the peoples of the world. The opposition he experiences brings him suffering and death, but in some deeply mysterious way his sufferings also bring forgiveness to the people who caused them, and he himself is rewarded beyond the grave.

Strictly speaking, this idea cannot be seen as part of the Messianic hopes of a typical Hebrew at the end of the Old Testament period. But Christians from the beginning have associated these poems with the Messiah, and so they must be included here.

The Hebrew belief in a Messiah, and the ideas associated with this belief, made it possible for the people to bear with their experiences in times of persecution and to discover God's presence as he worked out his Covenant and his final victory amongst them. Whatever the outward appearances might be, they knew themselves to be the people of the Covenant, and the powerful symbols with which they surrounded the idea of the Messiah expressed this fundamental confidence.

Chapter 9

HOW TO READ THE
OLD TESTAMENT

A Whole Library

The Old Testament is a whole library of books, not just one book, and like any library the books in it can be arranged in many different ways, to suit the needs of the readers. The books of the Old Testament are usually arranged in the order given to them many centuries ago, very like the order the Jews themselves used.

First they collected together all the information in their traditions about the early years of their nation, with the Exodus – the great escape from Egypt – at the centre. Then they added all their laws to that history, as if they had all been given to the nation by Moses. This made the first five books.

Then follow the history books about the Hebrews after they had entered Palestine, right through the years of the monarchy, the destruction of the two Hebrew kingdoms, the Exile in Babylon, and the restoration of the nation afterwards.

Next comes a collection of Hebrew literature, including the hymns sung by the worshippers at the Temple in Jerusalem. This part of the Old Testament ranges from works of pessimistic philosophy to love poems, and from collections of traditional proverbs to a play about suffering.

Finally come the writings of the prophets. Three of these, Isaiah, Jeremiah and Ezekiel, are mainly in the order in which the prophets lived (except that Isaiah's book also contains a great amount of material from later prophets whose names we do not know). The rest of the prophetic books are arranged in almost any order.

This is fine if you know a lot about it already, as any ancient Hebrew did, but it can be very confusing for a modern reader. Ancient interests can also be very different from modern ones, as a present-day reader soon discovers when he or she is faced with whole chapters of Hebrew family names, or detailed lists of the parts of Palestine which each Hebrew tribe occupied.

How the Old Testament Developed

The books of the Old Testament were actually written over a period of about a thousand years, in much the same way as English literature developed. Some people find it helpful to read them in the order in which they were written, so that they can see how the thought developed. This also makes it possible to see each book against the author's own historical background. It always helps towards understanding a book if you know something of the circumstances of the times when it was written.

There is no precise agreement amongst scholars about the details of such a chronological order for the books of the Old Testament, but readers may find the following suggestions helpful.

Early History and the Times of the Kings

First come the old stories about the first Hebrew ancestors, the escape from Egypt and the occupation of Palestine. These will be found in:

Genesis 12-50
Exodus 1-24, 32-34
Numbers 10-14, 20-25
Joshua
Judges
1 Samuel 1-7.

Then there is the story of the Hebrew kings, from Saul through to the end of the monarchy when the Babylonians destroyed Jerusalem:

1 Samuel 8-31
2 Samuel

1 and 2 Kings.

Some of the early literature, from the time of David and Solomon, is:

    Genesis 2-11 (parts)

    Proverbs 10-31

    Psalms, such as 28-31, 45, 80, 82, 132, 144.

Prophets from the times of the Hebrew kings, after 2 Kings 14, are:

    Amos

    Hosea

    Isaiah 1-12

    Micah

    Zephaniah

    Jeremiah

    Nahum

    Habakkuk

    Ezekiel 1-24.

Just after the beginning of Jeremiah's ministry, King Josiah seized an opportunity to reform the nation's life and religion, based on a revision of the law. This can be followed in:

    2 Kings 22-23

and the blueprint for the reform was:

    Deuteronomy.

The Exile in Babylon

Then followed the Exile in Babylon, after which there is no written history in the Old Testament. But there was a great deal of prophetic teaching, which can be found in:

    Ezekiel 25-48

    Isaiah 40-66.

Towards the end of the Exile, or shortly afterwards, the priestly leaders of the exiles assembled the first four books of the Old Testament from old traditions and inserted all the nation's laws, especially the laws about worship and sacrifice. They wrote an introduction about the creation of the universe:

Genesis 1 (and parts of Genesis 2-11)
and the legal material they added can be found in:
Exodus 25-31, 34-40
Leviticus
Numbers 1-10, 15-19, 25-36.

After the Exile

After the Exile, the restoration of the Hebrew nation is described in:
Ezra
Nehemiah
and the prophets of these times are:
Haggai
Zechariah
Malachi
Obadiah.
The priests wrote their own version of the nation's history during the monarchy (the same period covered in 1 and 2 Kings) in:
1 and 2 Chronicles.
The hymns sung in the Temple at this time, some of which date back to King David, are:
The Psalms.

Various Books

There remain various books which are very difficult to date because they have sometimes been attributed to famous men of an earlier period, such as King Solomon, to give them a special authority. Among these books are:
Job
Ecclesiastes
Proverbs 1-9
Ecclesiasticus
Wisdom
The Song of Songs.
Then there are stories which illustrate various periods of history, or political problems, such as:

Ruth
Jonah
Esther
Judith
Tobit
Baruch.

Finally, some books were written to encourage the Hebrew people in times of persecution. Such a time, which ended with victory for the Hebrews and a hundred years of independence, is described in:

1 and 2 Maccabees.

Examples of stories written at such times are:

Joel
Daniel.

The reader can start, of course, at any point in such a sequence of literature, if he or she wishes to read the Old Testament in this way. A more detailed version of this arrangement of the Old Testament, containing the material itself, will be found in *The Bible in Order*, by J. Rhymer.

Chapter 10

PEOPLE, PLACES AND IDEAS

Aaron Brother of Moses and spokesman for him in some of his confrontations with the Egyptian king. He is the ancestor of the main line of Hebrew priests, and accompanies Moses when he climbs Mount Sinai to receive the Covenant from God. (Exodus 4, 19, 28, Leviticus 8-10, Numbers 16-18)

Abel Second son of Adam and Eve, brother of Cain who murdered him. As a shepherd, Abel represents the pastoral peoples, who are traditional enemies of farmers, represented by Cain. (Genesis 4)

Abraham First historical ancestor of the Hebrew people, he travelled from Mesopotamia at God's command, about 1800 BC, to establish the first Hebrew links with Palestine. The covenants with Abraham anticipate the great Covenant with the Hebrews under the leadership of Moses. He is the father of Isaac, whom he was prepared to sacrifice to show his devotion to God. (Genesis 12-25)

Absalom King David's son. He rebelled against David and was killed while fleeing after his defeat by David's troops. There is a famous and beautiful lament for him, composed by David. (2 Samuel 13-19)

Adam The first man ('Adam' means 'man'), husband of Eve, father of Cain, Abel and Seth. He was made by God as the climax of the work of creation and given authority over all other creatures. His disobedience leads to all the disharmony and evil in the world. (Genesis 1-4)

Adultery Sexual intercourse in which one or both of the people involved is married or betrothed to someone else. It was a capital crime, punished by stoning to death. (Deuteronomy 22)

Ahab King of Israel (the northern Hebrew kingdom), 869-

850 BC, husband of Jezebel. He was attacked by the prophet Elijah for his support of the Baal religion and for the murder of Naboth. (1 Kings 16-22)

Ahaz King of Judah (the southern Hebrew kingdom), 735-715 BC. He made an alliance with Assyria, against the advice of the prophet Isaiah, introduced the Assyrian religion into the Temple in Jerusalem, and sacrificed his son by burning. Partly at his request, the Assyrians destroyed Damascus and the northern Hebrew kingdom, Israel. (2 Kings 16-17, Isaiah 7-12)

Alexander the Great King of Macedon, 336-323 BC. He unified Greece for the first time in its history, then defeated the Persians and created an empire stretching from North Africa to India, which included Palestine. His rule marks the beginning of Greek influences on Hebrew thought.

Altar A raised area where sacrifices were offered. The first Hebrew altars were a heap of rough stones or earth, but later altars were carefully constructed of dressed stone, wood, bronze or even of gold, and sometimes had projections shaped like horns at their corners. (Exodus 20, 27, Ezekiel 43)

Ammonites The eastern neighbours of the Hebrews throughout the Old Testament period, and usually at war with them. They lived in the highlands to the east of the Jordan valley. Amman, capital of the modern state of Jordan, is on the site of the Ammonite royal city. (Judges 3, 10, 1 Samuel 11, 2 Samuel 10-11, Nehemiah 4)

Amos A prophet. (See commentary on the Book of Amos)

Angel Literally, a messenger, and thus a messenger of God. Angels are mentioned as the guardians of people specially chosen by God, as servants who deliver God's messages and carry out his sentences of punishment, or simply as soldiers. In a famous vision, Jacob saw angels travelling between heaven and earth on a great ladder. In some of the earlier parts of the Old Testament, angels are mentioned instead of God himself, perhaps to protect the dignity and majesty of God. Later books mention seven angels who inspire the prophets and carry the people's prayers to God. (Genesis 32, Tobit 12, Daniel 8-9, Zechariah 1-6)

Anoint The sacred rite by which consecrated oil was poured on people's heads, especially kings and priests, to appoint them for special responsibilities. 'Messiah' means a person who has been anointed and given divine authority. (Exodus 31, 1 Samuel 10, 2 Kings 9)

Ark of the Covenant (See *Covenant Box*)

Ashkelon One of the five Philistine cities, on the Mediterranean coast of Palestine.

Assyria Mesopotamian power with its capital at Nineveh on the river Tigris. The Assyrians dominated Mesopotamia from 1100 BC and by the time of Ashurbanipal (668-630 BC) they had conquered most of the Middle East, including Egypt and Palestine. The Assyrians destroyed the northern Hebrew kingdom, Israel, in 721 BC, deported its people and replaced them with foreign settlers. The southern Hebrew kingdom, Judah, only survived by submitting to Assyrian control. Assyria was the most ruthless military power in the whole history of the Middle East. It was finally defeated by the Babylonians in 609 BC, who took over the Assyrian empire. (1 Kings 17-21)

Atonement The basis of this idea, in Hebrew thought, was cleansing from sin or defilement, normally by sprinkling a person or a place with the blood of a sacrificed animal. As the animal had been given to God, its life-blood contained special powers of cleansing from superficial sins. On the Day of Atonement, the high priest transferred the nation's sins to a goat, which was then driven into the desert. (Leviticus 16, 17)

Baal Literally 'lord' or 'owner', it was the name the Canaanites gave to their male gods. The Baals, together with their goddesses, were responsible for the fertility of the fields. The Baal religion was a fertility cult roundly condemned by the Hebrew prophets. (Judges 2, 6, 10, 1 Kings 16-18, 2 Kings 10, Jeremiah 11, 19, Hosea 2)

Babel One Hebrew version of Babylon. The Babylonian tower temples were the model for the Tower of Babel built in an attempt to reach heaven; the effort was frustrated by God. (Genesis 11)

Babylon Mesopotamian power with its capital on the river Euphrates. The Babylonians defeated the Assyrians in 609 BC and took over their empire. At first tolerant towards the Hebrews, the Babylonians lost patience with Hebrew intrigue, attacked and captured Jerusalem in 598 and 587 BC, and deported the people. On the second occasion they destroyed the city, including the Temple. The Babylonians were defeated by the Persians in 539 BC, who allowed the exiled Hebrews to return and rebuild Jerusalem. The 'Babylonian Exile' refers to the years when the Hebrews were forced to live in Babylonia. (2 Kings 24, Ezra 1, Jeremiah 20, 21, 24-52, Psalm 137)

Ban The custom of destroying enemy prisoners and property to show that the Hebrews must have nothing to do with their religion. (Joshua 6, 8, 10)

Baruch Jeremiah's secretary. (Jeremiah 32, 36, 45) (See commentary on the Book of Baruch)

Bathsheba Wife of Uriah, one of King David's officers, mother of Solomon. David first committed adultery with her and arranged for Uriah to be killed in battle, for which he was rebuked by the prophet Nathan. David married her and she became the most powerful influence in his life. (2 Samuel 11-12, 1 Kings 1-2)

Beersheba A town in the southern part of Judah with early Hebrew associations as a sanctuary. (Genesis 21, 26, 46)

Benjamin Youngest son of Jacob (Israel) by Rachel, who died giving birth to him. (Genesis 35, 42-46)

Bethel An ancient sanctuary just north of Jerusalem, specially associated with Jacob, who saw a vision of angels

there. When the Hebrew kingdom split after the death
of Solomon, Bethel became the chief shrine of the
northern kingdom, Israel. King Jeroboam erected a
golden calf there as a focus of worship, to the strong
disapproval of the Jerusalem priests. The prophet Amos
denounced Israel's sins at Bethel. (Genesis 35, Amos
3-5)

Bethlehem A small town just south of Jerusalem, the home
of David's family. Its associations with David led to the
belief that the Messiah would choose Bethlehem as his
capital when he came to rule Israel. The story of Ruth
is set in Bethlehem. (1 Samuel 16-17, Micah 5, Ruth)

Blood The life of animals, and therefore specially belonging to God. For this reason Hebrew law forbade blood
to be used as food, so it had to be poured on to the
ground when an animal was slaughtered. Blood had a
special significance in sacrifices as it represented life
charged with special powers from God. (Leviticus
throughout, especially 17)

Cain Eldest son of Adam and Eve, murderer of Abel. He
represents the farmers in their traditional enmity with
pastoral peoples. (Genesis 4)

Canaan The ancient name for Palestine, inhabited by people
with an advanced culture and social structure before the
Hebrews captured the area between 1200 and 1000
BC. The Canaanites were farmers who lived in fortified
cities, grouped in loose federations, and worshipped
fertility gods, the Baals. (Genesis 12, Joshua 3-17)

Chaldeans The founders of Babylon. (Genesis 12, 2 Kings
24-25)

Cherub The angel guardians of the Garden of Eden, and
of the Holy of Holies in the Temple in Jerusalem. They
are specially associated with storm winds, and sometimes carry God on his journeys. (Genesis 3, Exodus 25,
1 Kings 6, Psalm 18, Ezekiel 9-10)

Circumcision The custom of cutting away the foreskin
of a boy's penis eight days after birth. Originally a rite

performed at puberty to signify adult responsibilities, it became a sign of membership of the Covenant people of Israel, and thus an essential rite for all Hebrew males. (Genesis 17, Exodus 12, Leviticus 12, Joshua 5)

Commandments The most solemn form of law, especially the Ten Commandments given by God to Moses on Mount Sinai as the foundation of all Hebrew law and of the Covenant. (Exodus 20, Deuteronomy 5)

Covenant A solemn agreement between God and man, and especially the great Covenant made between God and the Hebrew people immediately after the escape from Egypt. This Covenant was then renewed at important points in the nation's history. Some of the prophets looked forward to a New Covenant, associated with the Messiah, which would succeed where the old Covenant had failed. (Genesis 6, 9, 15, 17, Exodus 19, Joshua 24, 2 Kings 23, Jeremiah 31, Ezekiel 17, 37)

Covenant Box The portable chest in which the stone tablets of the Ten Commandments were kept. It was carried before the Hebrew people on their journey through the desert from Egypt to Canaan, and subsequently kept in the Holy of Holies of the Temple built for it by King Solomon in Jerusalem. (Exodus 25-26, Joshua 3-6, 1 Samuel 4-7, 2 Samuel 6, 1 Kings 8)

Creation There are two accounts of the creation of the world in the early chapters of Genesis. The account in Genesis 1 is of late authorship and reflects developed thinking about the majesty and power of God. The earlier account in Genesis 2 is much less sophisticated. In each case the authors have drawn on material and stories in common use in the ancient Middle East, but they have changed them to avoid belief in many gods or any hint that God's power is limited. Apart from the opening chapter of Genesis, the most developed teaching about the creative powers of God and the way they are used is found in the later chapters of the Book of the Prophet Isaiah, which were written towards the end of

C

the Babylonian Exile, about 540 BC. (Genesis 1-2, Isaiah 40-66)

Cush Ethiopia.

Cyrus Persian king who defeated the Babylonians in 539 BC, took over their empire and encouraged the Hebrew exiles to return to Jerusalem. He financed their return and their work of rebuilding their old capital from Persian state funds, and gave the Hebrews protection against local opposition. So impressive was his help that he is referred to as 'God's anointed' in the second part of Isaiah (written by a Hebrew prophet contemporary with Cyrus). (Ezra 1-6, Isaiah 44)

Dagon A Philistine god. (1 Samuel 5)

Damascus Capital of Syria, the kingdom of the Aramaeans on the north-eastern frontier of Palestine. (2 Samuel 8, Isaiah 7)

Dan Son of Jacob and his wife Rachel's slave, Bilhah, and the name of one of the twelve Hebrew tribes. (Genesis 30)

Daniel Hero of a story of religious faithfulness set in the Exile period. (See commentary on the Book of Daniel)

David The first successful Hebrew king, successor of King Saul, he defeated the Philistines and united the Hebrew tribes. In 1000 BC David made Jerusalem the political and religious capital. His reputation as a poet and musician led to the authorship of the psalms being attributed to him. He founded the dynasty, through his first son Solomon, which ruled in Jerusalem without break until the city was destroyed by the Babylonians in 587 BC. His success and personality made him the popular model for the Messiah. (1 Samuel 16-2 Samuel 24, 1 Kings 2, Isaiah 7, 9, Jeremiah 22, 23)

David, City of Jerusalem.

Deborah A prophetess who led the Hebrews to victory against a Canaanite coalition. (Judges 4-5)

Decalogue (See *Commandments*)

Deuteronomy The fifth book of the Old Testament. (See

commentary on the Book of Deuteronomy)

Diaspora The general name given to Jews living outside Palestine. Their numbers increased rapidly from the Exile (587 BC) onwards, particularly in such cities as Alexandria and Rome.

Divorce In Hebrew law the husband had the right to divorce his wife with hardly any need to state a reason, unless he had falsely accused her of not being a virgin at marriage or had forced her to have sexual intercourse with him before marriage. There is no evidence about the frequency of divorce. (Deuteronomy 22, 24)

Eden The garden in which God placed man after creating him, and from which God then expelled man for disobedience. Later, it became a symbol for the restoration of man to God's favour in the Messianic age. (Genesis 2-3, Isaiah 51, Ezekiel 31, Joel 2)

Edom Neighbouring land and people south-east of Palestine usually controlled by the Hebrews. The Edomites helped the Babylonians to destroy Jerusalem in 587 BC and were the subject of a bitter psalm. (1 Kings 11, 2 Kings 14, Psalm 137)

Egypt The great power which occupied the parts of north-east Africa drained by the river Nile. Egyptian civilization was already more than two thousand years old at the beginning of the Old Testament period. The dependable flow of the river Nile, and its annual floods, made Egyptian crops far more certain than anywhere else in the Middle East. Egypt controlled Palestine until the rise of Assyria in the eighth century BC. The Hebrews settled in Egypt during a period of famine and were subsequently enslaved. Their escape in 1250 BC was the key event in Hebrew history, but the Hebrews looked for help from Egypt whenever they were threatened by other great powers. (Genesis 39-50, Exodus 1-12, 1 Kings 3, 2 Kings 18)

Elam A land in the mountainous area of north-east Mesopotamia. (Isaiah 11, Jeremiah 49)

Elders Normally the heads of families or of clans, they are representatives of the people who negotiate with the government, share some of its responsibilities such as the administration of law, and even affect the appointment of kings. (Exodus 3, 12, 18-19, 24, Deuteronomy 21-22, 25, 1 Samuel 8, 11, 1 Kings 8)

Election The belief that the Hebrew nation had been specially chosen by God. (Genesis 12, Deuteronomy 14, 2 Samuel 7)

Eli The priest of the central sanctuary, before Jerusalem became the Hebrew capital, where the sacred Ark or Covenant Box was kept. During Eli's time the Philistines captured the sacred portable shrine, and the shock killed him. (1 Samuel 1-4)

Elijah A prophet of the northern Hebrew kingdom, Israel, at the height of its prosperity. He condemned the prevailing Baal religion, and rebuked the kings for their injustices, at the risk of his life. According to 2 Kings 2 he was taken to heaven in a flaming chariot, hence the tradition that he would come again to prepare the people for the Messiah. (1 Kings 17-2 Kings 2, Malachi 4)

Elisha The prophet who was taught by Elijah and carried on his work. 1 Kings 19-2 Kings 13)

Emmanuel (See *Immanuel*)

Ephraim The second son of Joseph, and the name of one of the Hebrew tribes. (Genesis 41, Joshua 16)

Esau Eldest son of Isaac and Rebekah, brother of Jacob, who displaced him as Isaac's successor. He is the traditional ancestor of the Edomites. (Genesis 25-36)

Euphrates One of the two rivers (with Tigris) which drains Mesopotamia.

Eve Wife of Adam, created (according to the earlier of the two creation stories) from one of Adam's ribs. She was tempted by the serpent, and in her turn tempted Adam to disobey God. (Genesis 3-4)

Exile The period from 598-539 BC when the Hebrews of the southern kingdom, and particularly the inhabitants of Jerusalem, were deported to Babylonia. It was a particularly important time of reflection by the Hebrews on their history and their religion, and marked the end of the Hebrew monarchy. The restored Hebrew state was ruled by the priests of the Temple in Jerusalem. The first five books of the Old Testament, and most of the historical writings, were edited into the form in which we now have them during the Exile or shortly afterwards. (2 Kings 24, Jeremiah 27-29, 39, Ezekiel)

Exodus The escape from Egypt, about 1250 BC, under the leadership of Moses, which became the most important event in Hebrew history. (Exodus 1-15)

Ezekiel Prophet during the early years of the Exile in Babylon. (See commentary on the Book of Ezekiel)

Ezra Jewish leader after the Exile in Babylon. (See commentary on the Book of Ezra)

Fall The disobedience of Adam from which the Book of Genesis traces all human misery. (Genesis 3)

First Fruits The first gatherings of any crop at harvest time, which were sacred to God and so were offered to him in sacrifice. (Exodus 23, 34, Leviticus 19, 23)

Flesh The living body, especially human beings in their emotional aspects, and the members of a closely-related group of people. Of man in general, it refers to human weakness when contrasted with God's strength. (Psalm 63, Genesis 29, Psalm 136)

Forgiveness God's gift, through the Covenant, to those who confess their wrongdoing and ask for forgiveness, so that they are fully restored to the full privileges of the Covenant. It is particularly the mark of the New Covenant. (Psalm 25, Hosea 14, Jeremiah 31)

Gabriel An angel with special responsibilities for interpreting God's messages and signs. (Daniel 8-9)

Gad Son of Jacob by his wife Leah's slave, Zilpah, and name of one of the Hebrew tribes. (Genesis 30)

Galilee The northern part of Palestine at the head of the Jordan valley. The river Jordan flows from the Sea of

Galilee, an inland lake nearly 700 feet below sea level, and 13 miles long. (Joshua 20, 1 Kings 9)

Gath One of the five Philistine cities and home of Goliath. (1 Samuel 17, 21, 27)

Gaza One of the five Philistine cities which controlled the main coastal road to Egypt. (2 Kings 18)

Gerizim A mountain in the central highlands north of Jerusalem, site of an ancient Hebrew sanctuary. It was the scene for the renewal of the Covenant shortly after the Hebrews entered Canaan. (Joshua 8)

Gibeah A town just north of Jerusalem where King Saul met a group of prophets and shared in their ecstasy. (1 Samuel 10)

Gibeon A town just north of Jerusalem whose inhabitants tricked the Hebrews into making a covenant with them. (Joshua 9)

Gideon A Hebrew leader during the early years of settlement in Canaan, who led the people against Midianites who attacked from the desert. He refused to be made king. (Judges 6-8)

Gilgal An early Hebrew sanctuary somewhere near Jericho, from which Joshua began the attack on Canaan, and a meeting place for the Hebrews on particularly solemn occasions. (Joshua 4-5, 1 Samuel 13, 15, 2 Samuel 19)

Glory The outward sign of God's presence and majesty, and the reassurance of his protection. (Exodus 16, 40, 1 Kings 8, Ezekiel 1, 3, 8, 10, 11, 43, 44)

Gold The principal ancient sources of this precious metal were Egypt, Arabia and the eastern coast of the Aegean Sea. Egypt controlled the main supplies, and it was first imported into Palestine by King Solomon. (1 Kings 9, 10)

Goliath The Philistine champion from Gath who challenged any Hebrew soldier of Saul's army to single combat and was killed by the young David. (1 Samuel 17)

Goshen The north-east frontier district of Egypt where the

Hebrews settled. It was the place where the great coastal roads from the north entered Egypt and so was an important area for defence. (Genesis 45-50)

Habakkuk A prophet. (See commentary on the Book of Habakkuk)

Hagar Slave of Abraham's wife, Sarah, by whom Abraham had a son, Ishmael, when he found that Sarah was barren. (Genesis 16, 21)

Haggai A prophet. (See commentary on the Book of Haggai)

Ham Son of Noah, traditional ancestor of the Canaanites, Egyptians and Ethiopians. (Genesis 5-9)

Haran A settlement in the north of Syria on the main route out of Mesopotamia, the chief centre of the group to which Abraham belonged. (Genesis 11)

Harvest Festivals The three main harvest festivals in Old Testament times were Unleavened Bread, which marked the barley harvest; Pentecost, seven weeks later, associated with the wheat harvest; and Tabernacles, celebrated when the main fruit crops were gathered. These were Canaanite feasts which the Hebrews adopted and linked with their own feast of Passover so that they all became festivals of the Hebrew God. (Exodus 23, Deuteronomy 16)

Heart The centre not so much of the emotions as of the will, and thus the symbol for dedicated action. (Deuteronomy 15, Judges 5, Psalm 27)

Hebron An ancient city and sanctuary about 20 miles south of Jerusalem, Hebron was the main religious centre for the southern Hebrew tribes, and was the burial place of Abraham. (Genesis 13, 23, 35, 2 Samuel 2-5)

Hermon The highest mountain (nearly 10,000 feet) in the north of Palestine, and the northern limit of Joshua's conquests. (Joshua 11-13)

Hezekiah King of Judah, the southern Hebrew kingdom, 715-687 BC, who successfully defied the Assyrians on the advice of Isaiah, and briefly reformed his people's religion. (2 Kings 16-20, Isaiah 36-39)

Holy Literally, 'separate'. It therefore means 'uncompromising', 'objective'. God's decisions and his standards are absolute, and contrast with human standards, which all too often serve self-interest and the convenience of the moment. It is the key to God's power over the forces of evil and his utter condemnation of sin. The chief effect of God's holiness is the order or pattern for good which is the plan of the whole creation. Man feels awe or 'holy fear' when he recognizes God's holiness. Isaiah was overwhelmed by God's holiness in the Temple and it is the main theme of his teaching. Hebrew worship, particularly sacrifice, was the acknowledgement of God's holiness. (Exodus 28-31, Leviticus 16-27, Isaiah 6, Ezekiel 40-48)

Hosea A prophet. (See commentary on the Book of Hosea)

Immanuel Literally, 'God is with us'. The name given by Isaiah to the child whose birth was to prove to King Ahaz that Isaiah's condemnation of his decisions was true. (Isaiah 7-8)

Incense Aromatic gums and resins whose sweet smell when burned symbolized sacrifices and prayers rising to God. (Exodus 30, 35, Leviticus 16)

Isaiah A prophet. (See commentary on the Book of Isaiah)

Ishmael Son of Abraham by his wife Sarah's slave, Hagar, when Abraham thought that Sarah was barren. Sarah subsequently bore Isaac, and Abraham banished Ishmael and his mother. Ishmael was considered to be the ancestor of the Arabian tribes. (Genesis 16-17, 25)

Israel The name given to Jacob after he had wrestled with the angel, and so the name given to all of Jacob's descendants. After the split of the Hebrew kingdom at the death of Solomon, Israel was the name of the northern, larger Hebrew kingdom. (Genesis 32, 1 Kings 12)

Jacob Isaac's second son, who displaced Esau his elder

brother. (See *Israel*)

Jeremiah A prophet. (See commentary on the Book of Jeremiah)

Jericho A city at the northern end of the Dead Sea in the Jordan valley. It still depends for its existence and prosperity on abundant springs of fresh water. Situated at the foot of the main route to the centre of Palestine, and on an ancient crossroads, it was the key to Hebrew access to Canaan. Unfortunately, the excavations have failed to confirm the account of its capture by Joshua. (Joshua 2-6)

Jeroboam First king of the northern Hebrew kingdom, Israel, when the kingdom split at the death of Solomon in 931 BC. (1 Kings 11-15)

Jerusalem Capital of the united Hebrew kingdom created by King David in 1000 BC and of the southern Hebrew kingdom, Judah, after the split. Site of the famous Temple built by David's son, Solomon. Before its capture by troops of David's army, it was a Jebusite city. (See chapter 7: 'Jerusalem')

Jesse Father of King David. (1 Samuel 16-17)

Job The central character of an Old Testament book which discusses the problems of innocent suffering. (See commentary on the Book of Job)

Joel A prophet. (See commentary on the Book of Joel)

Jonah A prophet. (See commentary on the Book of Jonah)

Jonathan Son of King Saul. (1 Samuel 13-31)

Jordan The river and its valley which forms the eastern boundary of Palestine. It runs from the Sea of Galilee to the Dead Sea and is below sea level throughout its length. (Joshua 1-4)

Joseph Son of Jacob and Rachel, he was sold into slavery by his brothers and rose to high office in Egypt. His position gave the Hebrews the opportunity to settle on the borders of Egypt during the reign of sympathetic Egyptian kings. (Genesis 30-50)

Joshua Moses's successor who led the Hebrews into Canaan

at the end of the journey through the desert following the escape from Egypt. (See commentary on the Book of Joshua) (Exodus 17, Numbers 14, Deuteronomy 31, 34, Joshua)

Josiah King of the southern Hebrew kingdom, Judah, 640-609 BC, he initiated a great reform of the nation and re-newal of the Covenant, and was killed trying to prevent the passage of an Egyptian army through Palestine. (2 Kings 21-23)

Judah Son of Jacob and Leah, name of a Hebrew tribe and of the southern Hebrew kingdom whose capital was Jerusalem. (Genesis 29, 38)

Judges Military leaders during the early years of the Hebrew occupation of Palestine. (See commentary on the Book of Judges)

Laban Brother of Rebekah. (Genesis 24-31)

Law The whole pattern of God's relationship with his world, this is a much wider idea than law in the narrowly legal sense. The Hebrews called the first five books of the Bible 'The Law', because the history they describe and the creation of the universe all reveal the character of God, which is then reflected in the laws of the nation. (Exodus 19-24 shows this most clearly)

Lebanon The country immediately to the north of Pales-tine on the Mediterranean coast. It was famous for its cedar trees and was a centre of international sea trade from the ports of Tyre and Sidon. (1 Kings 4-5)

Leprosy Any contagious skin infection. The priests were given the responsibility of identifying it, and for decid-ing when a person had been healed. (Leviticus 13)

Levi Son of Jacob and Leah, and name of one of the Hebrew tribes. The Levites were particularly responsible for the organization of worship, and the Hebrew priests were members of this tribe. (Genesis 29, Numbers 1)

Leviticus Third book of the Bible. (See commentary on the Book of Leviticus)

Lord Usually the word which translates 'Yahweh', the

main Hebrew name for God. (Exodus 3, 6)

Love The voluntary commitment of one person to another, which was the most significant aspect of the Covenant between God and the Hebrew people. The whole of the Old Testament may be seen as growth in the Hebrews' understanding of the Covenant in terms of love. From the time of Hosea, love meant unselfish faithfulness, rather than a contractual relationship. (Deuteronomy 4-7, Hosea 2)

Malachi A prophet. (See commentary on the Book of Malachi)

Manasseh Joseph's eldest son and the name of one of the Hebrew tribes. (Genesis 41, 48)

Manna The mysterious food which God provided for the Hebrews during their journey through the desert after the escape from Egypt. (Exodus 16)

Marriage (See chapter 3 : 'Everyday Life')

Megiddo An ancient city in northern Palestine which commands the great coastal road as it branches inland towards Damascus and Mesopotamia. Solomon strengthened its fortifications. (Joshua 12, 1 Kings 9)

Melchizedek A king and priest, possibly of Jerusalem, who greeted Abraham and exchanged gifts with him. (Genesis 14)

Messiah Literally, 'someone who has been anointed with consecrated oil'. The rite conferred authority. The Messiah would be a leader sent by God with authority and power to establish God's kingdom on earth. (See chapter 8 : 'The Messiah')

Micah A prophet. (See commentary on the Book of Micah)

Michael An angel with special responsibility to guard the Jewish people. (Daniel 10, 12)

Michal Daughter of King Saul and wife of David. (1 Samuel 14, 18-19, 25, 2 Samuel 3, 6)

Midianites A nomadic tribe from the Sinai desert, to which Moses fled as a young man after killing an Egyptian official. (Exodus 2-4, 18)

Miracle The Hebrew idea means a task or an event which required strength beyond human or natural powers, and which must therefore have been performed by God. It can refer to an enormous range of activities, including the escape from Egypt, the creation of the universe, and God's judgements as they are expressed in historical events. (Psalms 9, 26, 40, 71, 72, 75, 86, 96, 98, 119)

Moab The small country immediately to the east of the Dead Sea, whose people refused to allow the Hebrews to pass through their territory during the journey from Egypt to Canaan. With the exception of a brief friendship during David's early years, there was normally war between the two peoples. Ruth came from Moab. (Numbers 21-23, 1 Samuel 22, Ruth)

Moses (See chapter 6: 'Moses, Architect of the Nation')

Naaman A Syrian officer whose leprosy was cured by Elisha. (2 Kings 5)

Naboth A man of Jezreel, unjustly executed on Queen Jezebel's orders so that her husband, King Ahab, could have Naboth's land. (1 Kings 21)

Nahum A prophet. (See commentary on the Book of Nahum)

Name Far from being a mere label, personal names in the Old Testament describe the character and position of a person. Sometimes a name was changed to fit a change of fortune. God's 'name' symbolizes all his powers and his relationship with his world, so to call on the name of God is to invoke his help. (Exodus 3, 6, 23, Psalms 20, 33, 54, 72)

Naphtali Son of Jacob and Bilhah, slave of his wife Rachel, and name of a Hebrew tribe. (Genesis 30)

Nathan A prophet at the court of King David who successfully rebuked the king for the murder of Uriah. (2 Samuel 7, 12)

Nebuchadnezzar King of Babylon, 605-562 BC, at whose orders Jerusalem was destroyed in 587 BC and the inhabitants taken to Babylonia. (2 Kings 24-25)

Nehemiah A governor of Judah after the Exile. (See commentary on the Books of Ezra and Nehemiah)

Nile The river flowing through Egypt, which was turned to blood in the first of the plagues of Egypt. (Exodus 7)

Nineveh Capital city of the Assyrians. (2 Kings 19, Jonah, Nahum)

Noah Tenth generation from Adam, father of Ham, Shem and Japheth, he was chosen to survive in the story of the flood with which God destroyed his evil contemporaries. (Genesis 5-10)

Numbers The fourth book of the Bible. (See commentary on the Book of Numbers)

Obadiah A prophet. (See commentary on the Book of Obadiah)

Oil Always olive oil, obtained by pressing the fruit of the olive tree. It was a most valuable product with a wide range of uses as food, medicine, the fuel for lamps and for cooking. (See also *Anoint* and *Messiah*) (Deuteronomy 28, 32, Isaiah 1, 1 Kings 5)

Palestine Strictly speaking, the country of the Philistines, but extended to refer to the whole region bounded by Lebanon, the Sinai desert, the Mediterranean Sea and the Syrian desert. It was the ancient land of Canaan.

Paradise (See *Eden*)

Passover The most ancient of Hebrew feasts, dating from their nomadic pastoral period as wandering shepherds. The main feature was the sacrifice of a lamb, whose blood was smeared on the tent or door lintels, and the roasted lamb eaten as a sacred meal. The Passover then became the feast commemorating the escape from Egypt under the leadership of Moses. (Exodus 12, Numbers 9, Deuteronomy 16, Joshua 5, 2 Kings 23, Ezra 6)

Patriarchs The founding ancestors of the Hebrew people, from Abraham to Joseph. (Genesis 12-50)

Pentecost The second of the harvest festivals, held seven weeks after Passover and Unleavened Bread. (Exodus

23, Deuteronomy 16)

Persia A country in the south of Mesopotamia which rose to great power under King Cyrus (559-529 BC) and defeated the Babylonians. (Ezra 1-4, Isaiah 44)

Pharaoh The title of the Egyptian kings.

Philistines Migrants who successfully invaded Palestine (which takes its name from them) from the sea and dominated the Hebrew people until their defeat by King David. (Judges 3, 10, 13-15, 1 Samuel 4-7, 13-31, 2 Samuel 1-8)

Plagues Particularly the ten disasters brought upon Egypt during the confrontations between Moses and the Egyptian king. (Exodus 7-12)

Priest The hereditary officials, members of the tribe of Levi, responsible for the system of sacrifices in Hebrew worship, the transmission of the nation's traditions and the making and administration of the law as God's will. The Hebrew priests grew in power with the developing importance of the Temple in Jerusalem, and the failures of the kings. After the return from the Exile in Babylon, the nation was ruled by the priests. As the people of the Covenant, the whole Hebrew nation was a community of priests. (Exodus 19, Leviticus)

Prophet The prophets were essentially teachers who showed the people of their own times the consequences of the Covenant and the nation's relationship with God. They have rightly been called 'the conscience of the nation', as they were prepared to condemn social injustice, and political or religious decisions which endangered the nation, no matter who was responsible. The prophets also taught the mercy and patience of God, and the attractions of responding to God's love. Only in a secondary sense do they 'foresee' the future, to show the consequences of present decisions and to emphasize the faithfulness of God.

Proverbs (See commentary on the Book of Proverbs)

Psalms The sacred songs sung by the Hebrew people, particularly during the worship in the Temple in Jerusalem. (See commentary on the Book of Psalms)

Rachel Daughter of Laban and wife of Jacob, mother of Joseph and Benjamin. (Genesis 29-35)

Rebekah Wife of Isaac, mother of Jacob and Esau. (Genesis 22-27)

Red Sea More properly, the Sea of Reeds. In the Old Testament, the north-westerly branch of the Red Sea, which peters out in a string of salty lakes and marshes to form the eastern border of Egypt. The passage of the Hebrews through this barrier, under the leadership of Moses, was the decisive moment in their escape from Egypt. (Exodus 14-15)

Rehoboam Solomon's son and successor as king, whose rudeness to the people of the northern Hebrew tribes provoked the split in the kingdom. He ruled the southern Hebrew kingdom, Judah, from 931 to 913 BC. (I Kings 11-14)

Resurrection There is hardly any mention of resurrection in the Old Testament. Elijah and Elisha both restored dead people to life again; the 'Valley of Dry Bones' passage in Ezekiel refers more to the restoration of the nation than to individual resurrection. The belief is expressed briefly in Isaiah and in the Book of Daniel. It would appear that most Hebrews did not hold this belief. (1 Kings 17, 2 Kings 4, 13, Isaiah 26, Ezekiel 37, Daniel 12)

Rome As Rome did not rise to power until the very end of the Old Testament period it is not mentioned, with the exception of an allusion to it in the Maccabee histories and Daniel. (Daniel 11)

Ruth Moabitesse and great-grandmother of King David. (See commentary on the Book of Ruth)

Sabbath Literally, 'the seventh day of the week'. The sabbath was set apart and all work forbidden, as a commemoration of the creation of the world and of the escape from Egypt. (Exodus 19, Deuteronomy 5)

Sacrifice Sacrifice was the main religious activity by which the Hebrews expressed their relationship with God. It was essentially connected with life, rather than death. Through sacrifice, the worshipper showed gratitude for God's gift of life in the crops, animals and human beings, especially the first-born and the first crops to be harvested. Blood played a prominent part, because blood contained life, and some sacrifices ended with a sacred meal in which the worshipper expressed his or her fellowship with God. (Leviticus, particularly chapter 17)

Samaria Capital of the northern Hebrew kingdom, Israel, from about 880 BC until its destruction by the Assyrians in 721 BC. (1 Kings 16, 2 Kings 17-18)

Samaritans Inhabitants of the region north of Jerusalem surrounding Samaria after the Assyrians deported the Hebrews and replaced them with settlers from the Assyrian empire. The Hebrews who returned from the Exile in Babylon refused to allow the Samaritans to help them to rebuild Jerusalem. (Ezra 4, Nehemiah 4)

Samson A military leader who unsuccessfully tried to rally the Hebrews against the Philistines during the early years of the Hebrew occupation of Palestine. (Judges 13-16)

Samuel A prophet and Hebrew leader immediately before the reign of King Saul. (See commentary on the Books of Samuel)

Sarah Abraham's wife, mother of Isaac. (Genesis 17-25)

Sargon Assyrian emperor, 722-705 BC, who established Assyrian control over Palestine and destroyed the northern Hebrew kingdom, Israel, in 721 BC. (Isaiah 20)

Satan In the Old Testament, one of God's servants who proves or tests the faithfulness of people. (1 Chronicles 21, Zechariah 3, Psalm 109, Job 1-2)

Saul The first Hebrew king, whom the young David served before Saul's jealousy turned the king against him. He died by his own hand during the battle in which he was defeated by the Philistines. (1 Samuel 9-31)

Sennacherib Assyrian emperor, 705-681 BC, who invaded Palestine and besieged Jerusalem, but failed to capture the city. (2 Kings 18-19)

Seraph The word is derived from 'fire', and refers to angels associated with flame and fire who attend God. (Isaiah 6)

Seth Son of Adam and Eve. (Genesis 4-5)

Sheba Part of Arabia, the modern Yemen, whose queen visited Solomon. (1 Kings 10)

Shechem An ancient sanctuary in the central highlands about 40 miles north of Jerusalem associated with the Hebrews from the time of Abraham. (Genesis 12, 33, Joshua 20, 24, 1 Kings 12)

Shem Son of Noah and traditional ancestor of the Semites, of which the Hebrews were a branch. (Genesis 5-11)

Sheol The place to which the dead go, where they remain in a shadowy and inactive existence. (Genesis 37, 42, 1 Kings 2, Job 21)

Shiloh An ancient religious centre in the central highlands which replaced Shechem as the main religious centre for the Hebrews before the foundation of the monarchy. (Joshua 18, 1 Samuel 1-4)

Sinai The barren peninsula formed by the two northern arms of the Red Sea. It contained the sacred mountain where the Hebrews received the Covenant from God during their journey from Egypt to Canaan under the leadership of Moses. (Exodus 16, 19-24, 31, 34)

Tabernacles, Feast of The last of the three great harvest festivals, when the fruits were finally gathered and the people camped in the fields. (Exodus 23, Deuteronomy 16)

Tabor A prominent hill near the coast in northern Palestine. (Judges 4, 8, Hosea 5)

Temple (See chapter 7 : 'Jerusalem')

Ten Commandments (See *Commandments*)

Tiglath-pileser Assyrian emperor, 745-727 BC, who established Assyria as a great power and began the Assyrian attacks on Palestine. (1 Kings 15-16)

Tigris One of the two rivers (with Euphrates) which drains Mesopotamia.

Tribe The earliest Hebrew organization, based on the family and dating from the patriarchs. The Hebrews were loosely organized in a federation of twelve tribes, with a central sanctuary situated at various places during the early years of their occupation of Canaan. The tribal organization survived the foundation of the Hebrew monarchy and in many ways competed with it. (Genesis 49, Numbers 1-2, 34, 36, Joshua 21)

Tyre Port and capital of Lebanon. (2 Kings 5, 7, 9)

Ur Chaldean city in southern Mesopotamia from which Abraham's family began their journey to Canaan. (Genesis 11, 15)

Uriah Husband of Bathsheba, murdered on David's orders. (2 Samuel 11-12)

Wisdom Practical skills, particularly in crafts and the art of government, rather than theoretical knowledge. (Exodus 28, 31, 35-36, 1 Kings 4, 10)

Zadok A priest who came to prominence after David's capture of Jerusalem, and was made chief priest by Solomon. (2 Samuel 8, 15, 1 Kings 1-2)

Zebulun Son of Jacob and Leah, and name of one of the Hebrew tribes. (Genesis 30, 35)

Zechariah A prophet. (See commentary on the Book of Zechariah)

Zedekiah The last king of Judah, the southern Hebrew kingdom, 597-587 BC, before its destruction by the Babylonians. (2 Kings 24-25)

Zephaniah A prophet. (See commentary on the Book of Zephaniah)

Part Two

COMMENTARIES ON THE BOOKS OF THE OLD TESTAMENT

THE BOOK OF GENESIS
Genesis 1-11

'How did it begin?'

Children want to know how their parents first met each other. The people of a great nation want to know about the pioneers who opened up new territory or fought for their freedom. The early days of a movement tell us a lot about the ideals of the people who gave their lives to it. In politics, the origins of a party help us to understand what it stands for now.

'How did it begin?' We ask the question because the way a thing began throws light on the way it is now. We want to know about our past, because we want to understand our present.

The Pattern of God's Plan

The opening chapters of the Book of Genesis are about beginnings: the beginning of the universe; the beginning of the world; the beginning of the human family; the beginning of strife.

They were written long after the events they describe. Indeed, those first, vital chapters were not so much 'written' as 'compiled'. They were put together by men who lived more than a thousand years after Abraham. By then, the pattern of God's way with his world stood out clearly. The Hebrew people could look back over the centuries of their nation's history, just as we can now look back over the centuries of British, American or European history. Like us, they could see something of the way it was all working out.

The events and circumstances of the past fell into a pattern. Whether the situation only concerned the family, or affected the whole nation, you could begin to see how people dealt with their problems. The pattern was not always clear, but enough of it was visible for writers to describe it so that other people could see it too.

It all makes sense when you see it in terms of God's almighty, creative power. It makes sense when you realize that God invites man to co-operate with him for the good of all the world. This is a story about distant beginnings buried deep in the past, but it is told so that people can understand the forces at work in their own times, and make the right decisions in their lives.

It is like a pilot who flies his plane at a great height, so that his passengers can see the way all the features of the landscape fit together. When they land, they will be plunged into the confusing details of roads and towns again, and have to find their way about. They will find it a great help to have seen the whole picture.

Shaping the Material

The men who compiled the opening chapters of the Bible worked with materials which were already to hand. Their materials were the traditions and stories handed down to them by earlier generations. Often the information had already been shaped by the prophets and teachers who lived before them. The prophets had been able to see God at work in the events of their own times. The events of the past had already been taught to people in language and stories which helped them to grasp the lessons to be learned. The whole mass of material was further shaped by the people themselves as they listened to the old, familiar stories and the accounts of past events.

Normally, they would be told to the crowds who had gathered at a sanctuary for one of the great religious festivals. Then the stories would help them to understand the worship they were offering to God. But the stories also belonged to the fireside and the intimacy of the home, as the family relaxed at the end of the day or on the sabbath. In either case, this is 'folk-wisdom' in the truest sense. It shows how a whole, mature people experienced God's power at work in their lives.

The stories used were sometimes ones which were known throughout the Middle East, such as a special tree growing in a sacred garden, or a flood in which only one man and his family survived. But the Hebrews changed the stories to fit the character of the God whom they had learned to know and worship.

In the other versions of the stories many gods appear, at war with each other, making war seem a natural, even a divinely authorized activity, rather than an evil. Two gods control the chaos from which the universe is made. Light is a god. The sun, the moon and the stars are all gods, so people thought (like many in our own times) that the stars and planets controlled people's lives here on earth.

The Hebrews would have nothing of this, so they changed the stories as they used them. In the opening chapter of Genesis God alone is the source of all that exists, and of all life and power. Chaos is only a formless mass of material, itself made by God, from which God then makes everything else. The sun, moon and stars are inanimate objects put there by God to give light and to help people to tell the time.

Only man is different from the rest of creation. Mankind was made, says the ancient Hebrew story, to co-operate with God and to administer the rest of the world. The human race would be the centre of the whole order of the universe, like the wise ruler of a nation, or the director-general of a great organization. With man at the centre, the rest of the universe would all fit into place in God's plan. The human race was given special gifts, so that it could do this special job. Man was made 'in the image of God', so that he could know how God thought, and administer his plans for the good of the whole creation.

The Mystery of Evil

With such a wonderful beginning, how could anything go wrong?

The answer is clear, however unpalatable it might be: the miseries and troubles of the world all come from man's refusal to fit into the plan himself. He insists on trying to be independent of God. He wants independent power to control everything else in God's creation. This is the significance of the 'tree of the knowledge of good and evil' and the fruit which man is forbidden to eat. In this sense, 'knowledge' is more than the innocent, useful learning and skills which the ancient Hebrews prized as much as we do. It represents the power to decide what is good and what is expendable. It means exploitation, suppression and ruthless domination for selfish ends.

Man's attempts to be an absolute power, independent of God, were bound to lead to confusion and misery. It was as if a country had two rulers with very different plans for the country's future; or like a ship with two captains who try to sail it to opposite destinations.

The Destiny of Man

The ancient Hebrew teachers and writers, who first told these stories, were throwing light on their own times. They were explaining the world in which they actually lived. It was a world in which families were divided and people were afraid of each other. Children were born in pain. Food was uncertain and difficult to grow. Man lived in an insecure and hostile world, pregnant with disaster.

If God is good, this cannot be the world he plans for those who have to live in it. He made man to live in communion with him, and to return his love with love. But love depends on freedom; it must be the free gift of the lover to the beloved, the free response of the beloved to the lover. And with freedom comes the risk that the freedom will be misused.

Those early chapters of Genesis lead into God's con-

demnation of the evil which man has brought into the
world. Again, the ancient writers used familiar stories
to convey the deep truths they wished to teach. A flood
destroys almost a whole, evil generation. Human plans
for world harmony, by building a tower to reach heaven,
are frustrated by God himself.

The world can be brought back to God again, but only
in God's own way. It seems a strange way, and slow. He
looks for a person who will respond to his call; someone
who will recognize him and obey him; someone who will
return his love.

It is a small bridgehead. At first it is only as wide as
one man and his family, but it will grow until it is an area
large enough to contain all the families of the world.

'Now the Lord said to Abram . . . . .'

The Founding Fathers
Genesis 12-55

God's People and the Great Powers

Every moment of every day, the news media remind us
that we live in a world which is dominated by great
international powers. Their policies and their decisions
reach across the world and penetrate into the smallest and
most remote of villages.

It is easy to forget that the ancient Hebrews were also
surrounded by great and powerful nations. They ruled
vast empires from their capitals in Egypt or Mesopotamia;
they were deeply suspicious of each other; they were
ruthless with weaker neighbours who occupied their frontier lands. The trade routes between Mesopotamia and
Egypt passed through Canaan, a narrow corridor of fertile land at the eastern end of the Mediterranean, which
we now call Palestine. It was to these parts that God
called Abram – soon to change his name to Abraham –

from an area more than a thousand miles away on the Persian Gulf.

At that time, the fertile parts of Canaan were farmed by people who lived in small, fortified towns, and Egypt controlled the area. But a nomadic shepherd people also passed through the area, moving with their flocks through the sparse pasturage of the hills. It was to these people that Abraham belonged. They lived by travelling, as their sheep ate the thin grasslands to the bare ground. They were the Hebrews.

Their way of life made them an independent people, for no place could claim them for long. They were a scattered people, for one flock could only support a limited number of families. In such a social organization, where the clan was the main unit, the head of the family was the true ruler of his people. At Haran, Abraham became head of his clan, and they moved slowly southwards with their flocks into the high pasture lands of Canaan. If famine struck, when their flocks were wiped out by drought, they could move to Egypt for a while, where the dependable flow of the Nile guaranteed supplies of food.

The Covenant

The men who collected the stories of Abraham, and wrote the Book of Genesis, lived many centuries later. By then they knew that it was all leading up to the great escape from Egypt and the Covenant of God which gave the Hebrew nation its distinctive character. In Abraham these writers were able to see the opening stages of God's plan, in which his initiative of love would be matched by man's response.

They described these early days in the language of the covenant: the relationship which God establishes with those who trust him. But Abraham was a man of his own times, when people expressed their devotion through crude and cruel means. He showed his willingness to give all to God, and to trust him completely, by making plans to sacrifice his only son, Isaac. Only at the last moment, with Isaac already bound to the altar and the knife raised to strike, did Abraham realize that this was not the way.

Five times the Book of Genesis mentions covenants between God and Abraham, and there are further covenants with Abraham's son Isaac, and with his grandson Jacob. Always it is emphasized that it is God who takes the initiative, so that there can be no doubt that it is his plan and his power which is at work.

In many ways, Genesis is a collection of stories about a very human family: its triumphs, its squabbles, its jokes and its mistakes. But running through it all is the guiding hand of God, until the people find themselves settled in Egypt, and the stage is set for the most dramatic and decisive moment in the whole Old Testament story.

From the call of Abraham to the time when the Hebrew people settled in Egypt was four generations, according to Genesis. It fits well into the pattern of Egyptian history as we now know it, for Egypt was captured by foreign, Semitic warriors about four generations after Abraham's time, who ruled for a hundred and sixty years. Such people would have no objection to nomadic Semitic shepherds settling just inside their borders, especially if one of the shepherds, Joseph, proved to be an able civil servant.

The scene was set for Exodus, the story of Moses and the great escape.

The Great Escape

THE BOOK OF EXODUS

Every nation has a moment in its history which captures the imagination of subsequent generations. Then people look back to that time for inspiration and comfort.

The Hebrew people look back to the great escape from Egypt, the Exodus, for their inspiration. It was then, more than at any other moment, that they were overwhelmingly convinced that God had chosen them. He saved them, guided them, and told them that they had a key part to play in his plan for the whole world. They were to be a holy people, a nation of priests, to show God to all peoples.

When they settled in Egypt, the Hebrews' response to the God of Abraham lost its first vividness, and the people sank into comfortable obscurity. They were saved by misfortune. They had settled in Egypt as the friends of foreign conquerors, the Hyksos, but a century later, the Egyptians expelled the Hyksos kings. The kings of the New Kingdom set about strengthening the frontier fortresses, and the Hebrews suddenly found that they were unwelcome foreigners living in a sensitive area of the country. The main military roads to the north, the invasion routes for Egypt's enemies, passed through Goshen, where the Hebrews had settled.

For the new Egyptian kings there was a happy solution to the problem. The Hebrews would provide the slave labour to build the new military bases for the frontier forces. Thus the foreigners would be controlled, and Egypt's defences strengthened. As the building programme neared completion, and the Egyptians felt that the Hebrews were still a security risk, they began to control their numbers by genocide. Male children were to be killed as they were born.

A Leader for the Times

But for one man, the Hebrews would have been absorbed or destroyed. They were saved by Moses, a Hebrew who by accident had been brought up at the Egyptian royal court.

He was in a unique position to help his people, but his actions show that he also had the qualities needed:
– He was a leader who could inspire people to follow and obey even when he led them into the most difficult situations.
– He was a prophet, with the truly prophetic gift of being able to see God at work in the events of his own times.
– He was a mediator, who could fulfil his people's need for a priest at this time of desperate need. He spoke for the people as they stood before God, led them in their worship and interpreted God's acts to them.

Moses was the man chosen by God to lead his people out of their slavery and turn them into the servants of God. The process would be as drastic as forging fine steel with furnace, hammer and anvil. Moses was to be the smith, inspired and guided by God. As always, God's saving power would be effective if there was an adequate human response. It was Moses who made this response.

Responsibilities

Moses learnt of his responsibilities in the desert areas east of Egypt, where he spent some time with a Midianite tribe of nomadic shepherds, who were fellow-worshippers of Yahweh, the Hebrew God. Moses learned about his father's faith amongst people who still lived in the desert, and it was in the desert that he experienced the presence of God in the mysterious phrase: 'I am who I am'.

It was a reassuring revelation, for it told Moses that God is utterly dependable, unchangingly concerned for his people's good. As the servant of such a God, Moses could not fail, provided he co-operated with God fearlessly and whole-heartedly. The promise of salvation would be honoured. Moses must tell the Hebrew people that the God of their fathers had sent him to save them.

Religion is seldom just a private matter, because our beliefs affect the way we behave towards other people. The rest of society may think that the beliefs of a particular group are a threat to security, or there may be economic repercussions if a group refuses to co-operate for religious reasons. Such problems were very real for Moses. Before he could free his people from their miseries he had to convince them that he could do it. If his plans failed, they would be even worse off than before.

The God-King

Moses had to get government permission for his people to leave, even for a short journey into the desert to worship the God of their fathers. In Egypt the government was the king, and the king was a god, for the Egyptians believed that their rulers were divine. The battle of wills between Moses and the Egyptian ruler turned into a trial of strength between two religions.

The famous plagues were the kind of natural disaster which struck Egypt from time to time, just as some areas are naturally subject to earthquakes, but the king interpreted them as attacks on his divine authority. Moses took the opportunity to convince both his own people and the Egyptians that the God of the Hebrews was more powerful than any Egyptian god.

The Great Escape

In the end the king was so convinced by the plagues, and frightened by them, that he did what Moses wanted. But it was the actual circumstances of the escape which proved to the Hebrews that their God was more powerful than all gods, and that he had chosen them to be his special people. Fleeing before a detachment of Egyptian frontier guards, the Hebrews came to the 'Sea of Reeds', the reed-filled marshes where a northern branch of the Red Sea peters out into a string of salty lakes.

Certain death seemed to face them, whether they went forward into the marshes, or turned to face the soldiers. But a strong east wind drove the water back in the marshy channels and Moses led the people across. When the Egyptians followed, their chariot wheels clogged, the wind dropped, and the returning waters drowned the armoured men as they floundered in the marsh.

The sight of their enemies 'lying dead on the sea shore' finally convinced the Hebrews. That memory was never forgotten, and it became the foundation stone of the nation's faith. They knew, now, that their God was greater than all gods. Soon they would realize that he was the *only* god.

The Covenant
The people's experience was sealed at the foot of a mountain, deep in the desert through which they travelled. God there told them, through Moses, that they must respond to the love that God had shown to them.

If the Hebrews were to be God's people, and his agents in the world, they must become worthy of him. All their laws and their behaviour towards each other must reflect the character of the God who had chosen them. Just as they depended on God's justice and love, so they in their turn must be equally just and loving in everything they did. It is no accident that the account of the Covenant in Exodus 19 is followed immediately by the Ten Commandments, and then by the earliest collection of Hebrew laws.

The Journey to Canaan
From now onwards in the Book of Exodus (and in the three books which follow it), the editors of this story make

the journey through the wilderness a framework for all of the nation's laws. Some of these laws belong to a much later period in the nation's history, but the authors of these books have inserted the laws here as a vivid reminder of the spirit which inspired them.

The law became for the Hebrew people a secure symbol of the love of God, for it shows that he cares about every detail of people's lives, and it tells them how they in their turn can show their love for him.

The Book of Exodus briefly resumes the story of the journey to the promised land in chapter 32, before breaking off again at chapter 35 for more laws about worship. The journey account is taken up again in Numbers 10.

The regulations about worship, with all the details of the size and shape of the altar, the furnishings and what the ministers are to wear, may seem tedious and unimportant to a modern reader, but these details show that worship was at the centre of the nation's life. If they placed God first, and took such care about his worship, they would have a pattern which would make sense of everything else that they did.

The teaching of the Book of Exodus is simple. The people have responded to the God who saved them from their slavery. If they are to make the most of the freedom which has been given to them, their God must remain at the centre of their lives. Whenever, in its later history, the nation forgot this simple truth, it was only by a renewal of the Covenant that it discovered itself again,

THE BOOK OF LEVITICUS

Glance through the television programmes scheduled for peak viewing time, or through the pages of any successful newspaper, and you will be sure to find that one type of programme figures prominently. It is the court-room drama, the legal case. Our attention is gripped because someone's life, liberty or reputation is at risk. The community's best brains and most persuasive thinkers are involved as judges and advocates. Whoever would think that law is a dull and dry subject?

The Pulse of the Nation

The law has an even deeper significance, quite apart from its importance for the person whose guilt or innocence is being put to the test. Beneath the surface of the law there beats the pulse of the nation. A nation's laws are a pointer to the values by which that nation lives. They spell out the right relationships between people. They establish ideals for the ways the members of the community should treat each other. The law expresses the principles by which a community lives.

For the Hebrew people, those principles were firm and clear, for they came from God. There was no compromise about them, and no uncertainty. Hebrew law reflected the character of the God who had chosen the Hebrew people, led them to freedom and made them into a holy nation. So it is no surprise that there are Hebrew laws which deal with the relationship between the people and their God. The largest collection of these laws is to be found in the Book of Leviticus, the third book of the Bible.

Holiness

Leviticus continues the regulations about worship which

have already been given in the later sections of the Book of Exodus. The details seem strange to a modern reader, for customs change in worship no less than in other areas of human behaviour, but the general principles are clear, once we learn to recognize them.

It is significant that the editor who collected together all the Hebrew laws has given first place to the laws about worship. Later books will spell out the law of human rights, family relationships, property and all the other aspects of community life, but first of all comes the law of God and his people, for all other law flows from it. If the relationship of the people with God is established firmly, all other relationships will fall into their right place.

So the first consequences of the Covenant between God and his people must be to safeguard the worship of God. It was the people's response to God's holiness.

It is impossible to define holiness, but it is easy to recognize it when you are in the presence of a holy person, or even when the atmosphere of a holy place makes its impact. Such a moment occurs in Isaiah chapter 6, which describes the experience in the Temple in Jerusalem which changed Isaiah's life. Isaiah says that he saw God enthroned in all his majesty, surrounded by heavenly beings who were worshipping him. His glory filled the building and flowed out into the whole world. The prophet was deeply afraid, and yet at the same time he could not flee. He felt utterly attracted, and he committed himself to this almighty being.

This is holiness. It is the power of God which breaks into the human situation from without. Its standards are absolute and impartial. It is detached from human compromise and from human imperfections. Yet it is concerned with every detail of human life as people struggle to live together in happiness and interdependence. Seen in this way, holiness is a wonderful principle on which to build a nation's laws.

The contents of Leviticus make best sense if they are

seen as a collection of laws gathered together by an editor many years after the escape from Egypt. Hebrew worship developed and grew, as the nation's way of life changed. The final editor has placed his collection here, and put it into the mouth of Moses, to show that these laws are all inspired by his spirit. The teaching which Moses first gave to the people, and the laws he himself made, set the pattern for all later generations.

Sacrifice

The collection starts with regulations for sacrifice, which was the most important part of Hebrew worship during the whole time of the Bible. During the final centuries of the Old Testament sacrifice was only permitted in the Temple in Jerusalem, but before that every village would have had its sacred place for sacrifices. As the laws show, every kind of human need, as well as the outstanding events in a person's life, had some kind of sacrifice associated with them.

The idea of sacrifice can be misleading if we do not take care to see it from the ancient Hebrew point of view. This way of worship was connected with life rather than death, as is shown by the significance attached to blood. The Hebrews believed that blood contained the life of an animal in a special way. When an animal was given to God in worship, its life-blood was filled with God's holiness and power. The worshipper then shared in that holiness by being sprinkled with the blood, as well as by sharing in a sacred meal. The death of the animal was only an incidental part of the ceremony and not the main purpose at all. In a similar way, flour and bread were sacrificed, especially if it was made from the first wheat or barley of the harvest, because this also was living food from God.

Leviticus then goes on to give instructions to the priests who officiate at the sacrifices, and the regulations for ordinations.

Next comes a strange section about animals which are

fit to eat and the ones which are forbidden. Reasons of hygiene may lie behind these distinctions, but there may also be strictly religious reasons. In some places, for example, the ancient inhabitants of Palestine worshipped pigs and other animals, so these prohibitions may have started as religious reforms. Such fundamental human concerns as childbirth, sickness and sexual relations all have their appropriate sacrifices. Once a year, on the Day of Atonement, special sacrifices were offered for the whole nation, priests and people. On this day, in a vivid piece of symbolic action, the high priest transferred the nation's sins to a goat, which was then driven off into the wilderness.

Justice and Compassion

The last part of Leviticus, chapters 17-26, contains a separate collection of laws, which the editor has added to the other laws, and these are sometimes called 'the Law of Holiness'. Many scholars hold that these chapters contain the earliest complete collection of Hebrew laws about worship.

In this holiness section the connection between worship and conduct is particularly clear. The holy God cares deeply about the well-being of his people, so they in their turn must show their holiness by their dealings with each other. Justice and compassion are sacred duties which reflect the character of God, for they flow from the worship of him. The power of God, which the people share in the sacrifices, declares itself through the quality of the nation's life. To ignore such power by committing social wrongs is to profane God's holy name.

THE BOOK OF NUMBERS

Journeys have a universal interest about them, so they make a natural framework for telling a story or teaching a lesson. The ancient author of the Book of Numbers evidently realized this, for half-way through his book, at 10:29, he starts the Hebrew people on their way from the sacred mountain towards the promised land of Canaan.

During half of the Book of Exodus (from Exodus 19), and all through Leviticus, the people are camped at the foot of Mount Sinai, where they received the promises from God and entered into their solemn Covenant with him. Exodus 34 describes the solemn renewal of the Covenant before the Hebrews resumed their journey through the wilderness after their escape from Egypt. The story of the journey is taken up again in Numbers 10:29-14:45 and in chapters 20-25.

Dangers

Twice during the journey the people are in danger from starvation and thirst, and in each case God saves them. Flights of quails arrived at an opportune moment, and Moses was directed to a hidden spring behind the surface of a rock-face. There he released the water by striking the rock with his staff.

But the most interesting incident is a Hebrew attempt to enter Canaan from the south. The journey from Egypt had taken them deep into the Sinai peninsula. Now they struck north for the promised land. Their journey should soon be over. A small force was sent to make a reconnaissance of the land, to report on the prospects and to estimate the strength of any opposition the people might meet. When they returned, the reconnaissance party brought back a vine branch with clusters of grapes. It was a prosperous country, they reported, 'flowing with milk and honey'. But they also reported that it was a country of fortified strongholds, with fierce and powerful inhabitants who would certainly put up a thorough defence against the Hebrew invaders. Against such prospects of spirited resistance, the Hebrews lost heart, and Moses interpreted their fears as rebellion against God. The ring-leaders of the rebellion were executed.

But the damage had been done, and a Hebrew invasion attempt was repelled. Moses told the whole people that they were not worthy to enter the land God had promised to them. They must now journey for a full forty years so that only their children would live to see God's promises fulfilled.

Later generations must have read many lessons into this incident. Not least, the Hebrew exiles in Babylon, seven centuries later, would be reminded that they must co-operate with God courageously and whole-heartedly when they returned to Palestine to rebuild the ruined Jerusalem.

Family Lists

Around this description of the first stage of the journey from Mount Sinai, the author of Numbers has arranged material of special interest to later generations of Hebrews. By the time he wrote, many of the Hebrew people were living outside Palestine itself, in the towns and cities of the Greek-speaking area at the eastern end of the Mediterranean.

All Hebrews (like people of any time or nationality) were interested in the history of their families, but the lists of names with which the Book of Numbers opens are of special importance. They helped later generations, and especially the Hebrews living in foreign countries, to identify with their nation. Hebrews living in foreign lands would be particularly proud of being descended from ancestors who had accompanied Moses on the great journey through the wilderness.

The lists of Levites are important, for the tribe of Levi provided the Hebrew people with its priests and ministers by hereditary right. The very authority of the priests and religious officials in later times depended in part on them being able to trace their family back in unbroken line to the lists of Levites in the Book of Numbers.

Then come various laws and customs, in no very obvious order, but some of them have special significance or usefulness for later generations. The regulations about trumpets, for example, in chapter 10, show that there was a special symbolism about the trumpet calls which sounded over Jerusalem whenever the sacrifices were offered in the Temple at the great public festivals. They recalled the journey through the wilderness, when God was leading his people from slavery to the freedom of the promised land. Whenever they heard the trumpets, the worshippers would know that God was still present amongst them to protect them by his holy power.

Moses's Successor

Towards the end of Numbers, in chapter 27, Moses names Joshua as his successor and gives him authority to lead the people by laying his hands on his head. It is a necessary act, because both Moses and Aaron will die before their people enter Canaan. Joshua will lead the people across the river Jordan, direct the conquest of their new country, and bring the whole enterprise to a successful conclusion with a solemn renewal of the covenant.

In the Hebrew war against the Midianites, which occurs next, there are startling accounts of Hebrew ferocity towards the people they defeated. Only girls below marriageable age were spared in the universal slaughter and destruction. Such accounts, both here and later, should only be accepted with caution. They were aimed at later generations who needed to be reminded of their duty to remain faithful to the Hebrew religion and traditions. Later Hebrew leaders were particularly worried when their people married foreign wives, who brought with them strange new faiths and customs. The native Canaanite fertility cult also had to be stamped out.

Some of the busiest trade routes in the ancient world passed through Palestine, and exposed the people to many other religious beliefs. Moreover, the Hebrews living in foreign lands were in particular danger of accepting the religions of the people amongst whom they had settled.

Allocation of Land

Finally, the boundaries of the promised land are defined in the Book of Numbers, and there is a very general allocation of the new country amongst the various Hebrew tribes. These details reflect the political situations more than 200 years later during the early monarchy, when David and Solomon imposed their rule over this area. But the boundaries are also those of a geographical area loosely controlled by Egypt, and in this sense it might be said that the Hebrews were settling in an outlying province of the Egyptian empire.

One practical detail reflects the compassion which Hebrew law showed, at least towards Hebrews. Certain towns were designated 'cities of refuge' and set aside for fugitives who were fleeing for their lives. They were afraid that the anger of their victims or of their families would overtake them before there was a chance of the law courts hearing the case and deciding it in a calmer atmosphere. The fugitive from blood vengeance would be safe in a city of refuge until his case could be heard. It guaranteed that no one would be punished until he had been proved guilty. There was to be no lynch law amongst God's people.

A Law for Living

THE BOOK OF DEUTERONOMY

It is safe to guess that everyone who reads these words has broken the law at some time in his or her life, and perhaps breaks it frequently. Such infringements need not be accidental ones, committed thoughtlessly or in ignorance. Sometimes they are deliberate acts, done because we think that particular law is a silly one, or for our own convenience. Even parking in a prohibited area, or staying there too long, is a breach of the law.

Keeping the Law

How do you get people to keep the law? Most of us would admit that it is through fear of being punished or humiliated if we are caught, at least in the case of 'lesser' crimes. But the best way is by showing people that the law makes good sense, and this is what the Book of Deuteronomy sets out to do.

At first sight, Deuteronomy is a strange book, for it repeats again many of the laws which have already been given in earlier books of the Bible. Moreover, those earlier books, like Deuteronomy, show Moses presenting those same laws to the same people. But the circumstances are different. This is the end of the journey through the wilderness. The Hebrews are camped on the eastern side of the river Jordan, ready to cross into the promised land. For Moses this is the end of the journey in another sense, for he is destined to die. Deuteronomy contains his last words of guidance and warning to his people, before they set out without him for their new life.

Gratitude

Moses sums up the nation's experiences during the journey

and reminds them that they have been uniquely blessed by God. God has chosen them, and proved his love for them through wonderful acts of power and deliverance. They must keep his laws to show their gratitude and to benefit from God's love. They will thus show the love of God, written on their hearts.

This is the setting for a repetition of the Ten Commandments, already given earlier in Exodus 20. There is only one difference of emphasis. In Exodus, the commandment to keep the sabbath, or seventh, day is a reminder of the creation of the world, when God rested on the seventh day. In Deuteronomy 5 it is presented as a reminder of the great escape from Egypt.

For a further six chapters, a second speech of Moses warns the people of the temptations they will meet in the new land, and reminds them of the laws God carved for them on stone tablets. Those laws are enshrined in the Ark of the Covenant, the sacred box which the priests carried before the people as they journeyed.

Then follows the main part of Deuteronomy, chapters 12-26, in which Moses expands those basic commandments into a whole legal code again, for the new way of life the people will lead when they cross the Jordan.

That is how Deuteronomy appears, and indeed it is a guide for the Hebrew people in their everyday lives as farmers in Palestine. But there is another way of looking at this book which shows even more strongly how valuable it became to the Hebrews at a time of crisis.

Blueprint for Reform

More than three hundred years after King David (and nearly six hundred years after Moses) the nation was in mortal danger. Corrupt kings had led their people into every kind of evil. The country was occupied by the Assyrians, and the Hebrews had willingly accepted the Assyrian religion. The nation had forgotten its vocation. A number of great prophets, including Isaiah, had tried to bring the people back to God again, but their teaching was ignored. Somehow, the vision with which Moses had inspired the founders of the nation must be revitalized.

Deuteronomy was to be the blue-print for the religious reform so desperately needed. It presented the people of a later generation with old, familiar laws, but for the first time it spelled out clearly the principles at the heart of each law. The people must keep these laws because their God had been so good to them, and they had accepted him as their God. They must feed the poor because they themselves had once been poor in Egypt. They must use their land and its produce to do the work of God, because it was given to them by God at a time when they themselves were helpless. They must remain single-minded in their love for God, because they still depended on his creative love for everything of value in their lives.

The prophets had taught all this before, but they had never related it clearly to the everyday laws which the people knew so well – and ignored. In this new form, the law could be seen as a positive blessing, a way of life which helped people to respond to God and to discover all that was best in each other. This was the way of life which the people had learned from Moses so long ago. Now, the author of Deuteronomy placed all this legal material, in its revised form, within the setting of the journey through the wilderness. And he put the laws into the mouth of Moses.

It was a vivid way of telling the people that this was the way Moses would have guided them if he had been their leader now. And it showed the people that the God who had saved their ancestors from slavery in Egypt could still save them, now that they were enslaved to a corrupt way of life.

The End of an Era

There is no sure way of knowing which of these two views of Deuteronomy is historically correct. It may well have been what Moses taught the people immediately before they entered into the promised land. But it is more likely that it was a particularly vivid and successful way of reminding a later generation that they had lost the inspiration that Moses had first given to their nation. If this second view is the correct one, an account of the dramatic reform inspired by Deuteronomy can be found in 2 Kings chapters 22-23. On either view, it is appropriate that Deuteronomy ends, in chapters 32 and 33, with two long and very moving songs.

The first is a great hymn to the wonderful love of God and his saving power. If the poem also exults triumphantly over the downfall of the Hebrews' enemies, it is only because this is also one way in which the people acknowledged God's greatness.

The second poem is a lingering, affectionate blessing by Moses of the tribes he had led on their long journey from slavery to freedom. One by one they are all named, and described in all their varied characters, like a father reflecting on the children he loves. The language suggests that it is a very old poem, dating, perhaps, from the very time when the Hebrew people entered Canaan after the death of Moses.

That momentous death marks the end of the most dynamic period in the whole history of the Hebrew people. It provides an appropriate close for the Book of Deuteronomy, and for the great sweep of history which opens at the beginning of the Book of Genesis with the creation of the world.

Taking Possession

THE BOOK OF JOSHUA

With the Book of Joshua, the Bible starts the long history of the Hebrew people in the promised land.

The story begins with the moment when the people crossed the river Jordan at the end of their long journey through the wilderness. God had rescued them from slavery in Egypt and made a special covenant with them. Now they were ready to start the new life God had planned for them. Every detail of their lives in the new land must mirror the God who had given it to them.

The story ends more than a thousand years later, with the nation safe again after invasion, devastation, exile and desperate struggles to preserve its unique religious tradition. We have to bear this background in mind as we read these books of history. For they are not history as we now expect history to be told. They are written to reassure and inspire people of later generations. So the events described have been selected to serve this special purpose, and the authors touched up the story if this helped to point the moral.

Ambassadors

The people who wrote this history were conscious that God had chosen their nation for a special purpose. They were to be his ambassadors to the world. For such a wonderful and frightening responsibility, they must first be faithful to God in their own lives.

Above all, this is history seen through the eyes of faith. If the reader does not accept the point of view of the people who are telling the story, it will seem crudely nationalistic and arrogant.

In one respect, at least, the Book of Joshua presents us

with a reliable picture. The land of Canaan was already peopled when the Hebrews entered it. The Canaanites were farmers, who lived in fortified towns and villages, and farmed as much land as they could safely reach from their strongholds. The country was dotted with such settlements wherever there was fertile land, and with religious sanctuaries. Each large town had a king, who ruled his people with absolute power, a servant of the gods who controlled the fertility of the land and of the crops it bore.

There were real dangers to the Hebrews in the Canaanite way of life. The Canaanites had a rigid system of social classes, with different laws and privileges for each class. This idea clashed with Hebrew beliefs in freedom and the equality of everyone before God's law. Then again, the Hebrews believed that their God was the creator of all things and the source of all life. It would be fatal if they accepted a whole system of Canaanite gods who controlled the farmers' life of sowing, growing and harvesting.

Faithfulness

Throughout their history, the Hebrews had to be reminded of their unique religion, and encouraged to return to it when they had neglected it or turned to other beliefs. The Book of Joshua is just such a reminder. It presents an idealized picture of the conquest of Canaan. Whenever the people were strictly faithful to God, they were victorious. When they compromised, and flirted with Canaanite ways, disaster overtook them. Strict faithfulness to God is symbolized by orders to be ruthless towards Canaanites and their property. All must be destroyed, people and possessions.

The conquest itself is described as a lightning campaign in which the Hebrews first captured Jericho with the aid of the sacred Ark, the Covenant Box, and the trumpets blown by the priests at the sacrifices. Then the victorious people of God fanned out through the country and established their control over it. The campaign is more a symbol of God's power than a reliable description of history. In fact, the next book, the Book of Judges, is a more convincing account of the Hebrew occupation of Canaan, as will be seen.

A closer examination of the Book of Joshua shows that it is mainly concerned with the territory occupied by the tribe of Benjamin, just north of Jerusalem. (Jerusalem itself did not become a Hebrew city until the time of David, more than 200 years later.) This mountainous region had only a few Canaanite settlements, which were quickly overcome. The only place of any size would be Jericho, deep in the Jordan valley just north of the Dead Sea. Then, as now, Jericho only existed because of abundant springs of fresh water, which make it an oasis in that hot and barren region.

Excavations have confirmed that the ancient city of Jericho was large for the times, and protected by massive walls. Unfortunately, they have not confirmed that the site was fully occupied with intact fortifications when the Hebrews crossed the Jordan into Canaan.

Title Deeds

The second half of the Book of Joshua contains long lists of towns occupied by the various Hebrew tribes, together with the boundaries of the tribal territories. Here we may see another function this book performed for later generations. It served as a collection of title deeds of property for the Hebrew tribes and the families who belonged to them. Land divisions rested here on divine authority.

The renewal of the Covenant, with which the book ends in chapter 24, is important. At every stage in the nation's history the people needed to remember and to renew their Covenant with God. They had to realize that his creative power is present throughout the nation's life, and in every detail of it, not just at the beginning of its history. The solemn renewal of the Covenant became a regular feature in the nation's life, whenever there was need for reform, and a strong leader emerged who was prepared to bring the people back to God again. Joshua's renewal of the Covenant was a model for later generations.

But for all the doubts we may have about the Book of Joshua as strict and literal history, there is one central truth that runs right through its descriptions of events. God's power is available to all the people, to the weak and the insignificant as well as to the leaders and the great, but it is only effective when it is recognized and accepted responsibly. It is a real Covenant. God's people are his partners in his work, not his tools.

Out of such a relationship comes love. There is a real risk of rejection and failure when men choose their own selfish ends and their own selfish ways of achieving them. But when they do co-operate freely and whole-heartedly with God, his love proves greater than any obstacle in their path. Later generations of Hebrews needed that re-assurance as much as we do. The Book of Joshua gave it to them.

THE BOOK OF JUDGES

History has many lessons to teach us, but the history must be convincing if it is to teach us anything. The Book of Judges is less exciting, but it is more convincing than the romantic picture given us by the Book of Joshua.

Both books deal with much the same period in Hebrew history, the early years when the nation was gaining control of Canaan. Joshua pictures it all as a swift and dramatic conquest. Judges describes a slow and painful process, with many set-backs, where occupation of the land is achieved by infiltration more than by decisive victories.

The period described extends from the entry of the Hebrew people into Canaan until very nearly the time when they elected their first king, Saul. This is a little less than 200 years, but it covers a time when the Hebrews were having to change their way of life from travelling shepherds to settled farmers. This was an enormous change, comparable with the change in Britain or the United States during the Industrial Revolution, from an agricultural way of life to a technological one. The Hebrews entered Canaan as semi-nomadic shepherds with a way of life based on closely-knit family units. Within 200 years they had become an agricultural people, living in fortified villages, with the beginnings of a central organization to regulate their worship and to administer justice.

Strong Leaders

There were many crises, and the Book of Judges mentions some of them. The most serious danger came towards the end of the period, when the Philistines succeeded in gaining control of most of Palestine, and it became clear to the Hebrew people that they would have to give up some of their independence if they were to shake off Philistine control.

The Judges are not really judges in our sense of the word, for their main job was not connected first of all with the administration of justice. They were essentially strong men, who emerged in moments of crisis as leaders who could rally the people and gain victory against the enemy which was threatening them. After the victory had been secured the leaders continued to be important men in the community, to whom people would go if there was a dispute which could not be settled by the local village elders.

Law and Authority

The law which they administered as judges was the law of common sense. It was case law based on precedents and the kind of thinking which a man would give as he considered a problem and circumstances calmly, and discussed it with the other leading people in the community. Yet all the time he would have in mind the principles of the Covenant which God had made with his people and which guaranteed their freedom and their equality.

During this period the sacred Ark, the Covenant Box, was kept at a central sanctuary, and the priests who looked after the Ark provided the beginnings of a central authority. It was nothing like the kind of central government with which we are familiar, or even like the kind which emerged when the monarchy was established in Israel. There was no civil service; the people depended on their local leaders and worshipped at their local sanctuaries.

Early in the Book of Judges there is a description of a campaign against a coalition of Canaanite cities, in which the Hebrews were led by a woman, Deborah. The Canaanite general, Sisera, was murdered in his sleep. The story connects God with treachery and sheer military power, and has very little in it which we might recognize as religious. It ends with a very old Hebrew song of victory, which contains passages of ruthless delight in the destruction of the enemy. The Hebrews have a long way to go before they realize that God is reaching out into all his world through them, to draw all peoples into his love.

A period of peace followed and then the people were again threatened through the reigns of the nomadic Midianites. By this time the Hebrews had begun to worship the Canaanite fertility gods, and the struggle, led by Gideon, symbolizes the struggle against the Canaanite way of worship.

The Need for Security
There is an interesting passage here in which Gideon refused to become king, that is, a permanent ruler who would hand on his authority to his son. Here we have the first indication that the people felt the need for a stable form of government which would organize a more effective defence against enemies and give the people real security. Gideon's sons did in fact rule after him, and there is a hint in the text that they abused their rule.

With the collection of stories about Samson in Judges chapters 13-16, the most serious enemy that the Hebrews had to face during this period comes on to the scene. This was the Philistines. They came by sea across the Mediterranean at the end of the 13th or the beginning of the 12th century BC. They had attempted at first to invade Egypt, but the Egyptians repulsed them in a series of bloody battles in the channels of the Nile Delta. They then founded five cities straddling the coast road through southern Palestine, and pushed out into the territory occupied by the Hebrews and Canaanites. Very little is known about the Philistines, except that they were the last wave produced by a series of migrations which began somewhere in the heart of Asia.

Whole nations migrated westward and southward, and created pressures which forced out the people who were living in the Greek islands or the Balkans. Amongst those people were the Philistines, and they sailed eastwards and landed in Palestine. In fact, the very name Palestine comes from the Philistines. So successful were they at first that they gave their name to the region.

Philistine Control
The Philistines were united together in a loose federation based on their five cities, each of which had a king, but in times of war they elected one of the kings as their military leader. They were amongst the first people to use iron in their weapons and agricultural tools, and this may well account for their successes against the Hebrew people. Naturally enough, they kept a close control over the use of iron amongst the people that they conquered, including the Hebrews.

It was a situation which could not last. Even Samson was powerless in the end against the Philistines. The old, loose tribal organization would have to give way to a more permanent authority if the Hebrews were to survive as a nation. First Samuel, and then Saul tried to fulfil this need, but neither of them succeeded.

The people would have to wait until an obscure shepherd boy was called to lead them, and make the name of David echo down the centuries.

Happily Ever After

THE BOOK OF RUTH

At first sight the Book of Ruth appears to be simply a charming short story, containing a message of compassion for the alien and the stranger. It tells of Naomi, widowed in a foreign land, whose two sons both died. Their wives, Orpah and Ruth, were non-Jews, Moabites. Naomi decides to return to Judah and tries to persuade her two widowed daughters-in-law to stay in their own land. Orpah agrees. But Ruth says:

> Don't ask me to leave you. Let me go with you. Wherever you go, I will go; wherever you live, I will live. Your people will be my people, and your God will be my God. Wherever you die, I will die, and that is where I will be buried. May the Lord's worst punishment come upon me if I let anything but death separate me from you! (Ruth 1:16-17)

Back in Judah, Ruth follows the harvesters in the barley fields of Boaz and, as the law allowed, gleans what they leave behind. Naomi encourages Ruth to seek marriage with Boaz and eventually, after some difficulty, Ruth and Boaz are married. Their marriage is blessed with a child and all live happily ever after.

The Moral of the Story

This short story was written some time after the Jews had returned from exile in Babylon. It was a time of national reform inspired by the scribes Ezra and Nehemiah (see pages 136-139), though the reform was marred to some extent by a fierce nationalism which produced an apartheid-like prejudice against all non-Jews.

The story of Ruth may have been told as a gentle rebuke at this narrowness of outlook, for in the last few lines, very subtly inserted, appears the moral of the story. Ruth's son was named Obed. 'This was the father of David's father, Jesse', the story-teller quietly concludes. David, of course, was the great national hero, and here we are told that his great-grandmother was an outsider, a non-Jew. It is as if a story were told about some remote unknown coloured or black woman living in South Africa one hundred years ago, and the writer were to end by saying 'And this woman was the great-grandmother of our President!'

The Making of the King

THE FIRST AND SECOND BOOKS
OF SAMUEL

Government means power. It means giving men power over their fellow men: power to give their country peace and security and the opportunity for everyone to make the most of their lives, but also power to send people to gas chambers or to bomb a whole country into ruins.

It isn't enough that a government is strong, or even that it has the support of the majority. It must also be good, searching out the right thing to do even when it is unpopular, and always aware that the people whom it governs are the children of God.

King David had all the potential to be such a good ruler. Attractive, able, confident, he arrived on the scene just when his people needed him. He inspired a deep loyalty in those who worked under him, he risked his life to defeat the nation's enemies, and he made good, clear political decisions which brought prosperity after victory.

Yet in his moment of secure triumph he came near to bringing the whole achievement into stark ruin by an act of uncontrolled selfishness. If he had been allowed to get away with it he would have dragged all his people down with him. In the end David learned to govern as God's agent, but it was the last of his lessons in kingship, and it took a prophet to teach it to him.

Submission to Force

1 and 2 Samuel are the books which tell this story. In fact, it would have been more accurate to have called them 1 and 2 David.

Shortly after the Israelites escaped from Egypt and entered Palestine from the east, another group of people landed from the sea and spread into the land from the west. These were the Philistines, or 'the sea people' as the Egyptians called them. They settled on the great coastal road which runs up Palestine, and then they extended their control right through to the river Jordan. At first they were successful, and the Hebrews found themselves ruled by the Philistines.

A critical battle was fought near the coast at Aphek, and when the Hebrews found they were losing they fetched the sacred Ark, and carried it before them into the battle. But the Philistines fought with renewed determination and the sacred Ark itself was captured. So complete was the Philistine victory that they were able to force the Hebrews into complete submission.

During these years, the prophet Samuel led the scattered Hebrew people, but it is clear that the task was beyond him. Indeed, the situation was more serious than any the Hebrews had yet faced, and in the end it changed the whole life of the people.

It also brought to a head the problem of how a ruler should behave. The people of God found peace and unity by making a king, but they could only be God's people if the king himself ruled in the way God wanted him to. The experiment came near to ending in disaster at the very moment of triumph.

Samuel

The stories about these years have come down to us, in 1 Samuel, from two traditions, so sometimes there are different versions of the same incident. In one of the traditions the most important person is the prophet Samuel, who is presented as king in all but name. When the people asked Samuel to make Saul their first king, Samuel warned them that it would mean that they had turned away from God. In this version Saul's death in battle became the proof that Samuel was right.

There is, however, another version, and in this one

Saul comes to the front, like any other leader, to rescue his people from the tyranny of the Philistines. In this he was very nearly successful, but two things marked Saul out from the other leaders who came before him. One is the fact that the people made him a king, and the other is that David rose to power during his reign.

The people longed for stability, and perhaps they also wanted a symbol of their national pride, a king who could send ambassadors and be famous abroad. But the request was full of dangers: a temporary leader could be dismissed or ignored if he was unsuccessful or became tyrannical; deposing a king was a different matter altogether.

Greater still was the danger that the people would forget their need for God. So far the nation had been held together by the miracle of their escape from Egypt. The memory of this might fade if they had a king to lean on, and kings at that time had a habit of turning themselves into gods.

David and Goliath
David enters the story as a young man not even old enough or important enough to serve in the army fighting the Philistines. He arrived at the front with food for his brothers, and found that one of the Philistines, Goliath, had challenged the Israelites to send a champion to fight him alone in front of both armies. Whichever man won would fill his watching army with confidence. No man from Israel would take the risk.

Filled with shame by the timidity of his countrymen, the young David persuaded King Saul to let him take up the challenge. The unencumbered boy with a sling had all the advantages of mobility over the heavily armed soldier, and he used his advantage to the full. Goliath was stunned by a stone, and David swiftly finished him before he could regain consciousness. The challenge had been met. The wavering Hebrew army roared into battle and forced the Philistines back to their coastal cities.

David the Outlaw

It seemed that David's future was assured. Saul gave him command of the royal bodyguard, he became the closest friend of Saul's son, Jonathan, and he could do no wrong. Yet his very success was his chief danger, for people sang that David was a greater warrior than Saul, and King Saul suddenly saw David as a threat to his own authority.

David could no longer feel safe at the royal court, so he fled. In his jealousy and fear Saul showed that he would stop at nothing. Early in his flight David was helped by the priests in the city of Nob. Saul ordered his men to slaughter all the people of the city. Only one escaped to join David in his years of exile, and serve the outlaw band as priest.

The next few years were vital for David. He knew that he could rule the people more surely than Saul could, yet he dared not interfere. If he helped overthrow Saul he risked committing blasphemy, for Saul had been made king in the name of God. Besides, all the northern group of Hebrew people supported Saul, and David would need their loyalty later.

For much of the time David lived the life of an outlaw, hunted by Saul and fleeing from one hiding-place to another. In the end, however, David was bound to be caught, and he could look for no mercy from Saul, no matter how often he himself had spared Saul's life. He fled with his followers to the Philistines, and was welcomed by them as an enemy of Saul. Fortunately, he did not have to fight Saul, for some of the Philistines were still suspicious of him, and would not let him go into the battle.

Saul and Jonathan were killed, and David was able to mourn them in all sincerity. The way was clear for him to unite all the Hebrew people under his rule.

David the King

Gaining the loyalty of the scattered Hebrew tribes called for all the diplomatic skills that David could command, but he succeeded, and the way was clear for him to defeat the

Philistines and confine them to the coastal area.

The people now needed a central symbol which would express their unity as a nation and give them a focus. The old tribal organization no longer met their needs. They had changed, in fact, from being a wandering people and had settled as farmers. A whole new social structure had evolved and needed to be consolidated.

It is the real genius of David that he chose a new capital as the central symbol for the Hebrew people. Thus Jerusalem became the inspiration for the Hebrews from David's time until today.

It was a good place for a capital. It was central, and it did not belong to any one group of the Hebrew people, so there would be no jealousy amongst the rest. Moreover, on its narrow ridge, with a good supply of water, the city could be made impregnable. David's men captured it through an unguarded water tunnel, and he set the seal on his new reign by then leading the united people against the Philistines and defeating them decisively. David moved the sacred Ark, the Covenant Box, to Jerusalem, to show that God was once more at the centre of the nation's life.

Everything seemed set for a glorious future. The people's desire for a stable government, respected and honoured and feared by the surrounding nations, had been fulfilled. In a very important passage in 2 Samuel 7, the old Covenant with God was re-interpreted. King David was now the guardian of the Covenant between God and his people, and the line of kings which would descend from David would take up the responsibility, each in his turn.

The Test of Kingship

But the king had still to learn what it meant to be king over God's people. For his power was limited : he must use it in the way God wanted. His rule must be God's rule.

David's harshest lesson was to learn that the greatest danger to his people lay not in any enemy outside, but in David himself. He had great power, but it still wasn't clear whether he would use it to lead his people to God or to drive them away from him.

The critical moment in David's rule came very soon after he had united the people and made his throne secure. David became involved with the wife of one of his officers while the army was away on campaign. When the woman, Bathsheba, became pregnant by him, and the unsuspecting husband would not co-operate in David's plans to disguise the scandal, David had him murdered. David then married Bathsheba. It was a hideous act of treachery, but it was more than that, for it was a betrayal of the God who had brought his people out of Egypt.

In the Covenant, and in the law, God had taught that mere power is not enough. If the power is not used rightly it is no longer God's power. If the king himself, ruling as God's agent, misused his power, rot would spread throughout the nation. If David failed, everyone with any power at all over his fellow men would think he could use it as he liked. The example of the king, good or bad, set the tone for the whole of the new kingdom. It was a moment of the utmost importance in the unfolding of God's plan to bring his world into his love.

Confronting the King

It fell to Nathan, the prophet, to bring home to David the horror of what he had done. It was a difficult task. David had only acted as any other king of his time might have done, for many of the surrounding peoples thought of their kings as gods who could in practice do what they liked with the lives and property of their subjects.

Nathan pretended that he had a case of theft to bring before the king. David gave judgement and Nathan then told him that he was the man who had committed the theft. David took the point, and by public repentance made it plain to his people that this was not a kingdom where there was one law for the king and another for the people.

God's standards of right and wrong were the kingdom's standards.

It was an important moment in another way, too. Saul and David had had advisers who could help them to come to decisions, but they had never had anyone who would confront the king and tell him to his face that he was wrong. There had never been a king's conscience. Nathan is the first of the long line of great prophets who could see the nation's affairs from God's point of view and were not afraid to speak out. From now on the prophets would look on their own times from God's standpoint and tell the people plainly what they saw.

The rest of David's reign was a personal tragedy. His favourite son, Absalom, murdered another of his sons and the whole incident blew up to a full civil war. In the end Absalom was killed, but not before David had had to flee for his life from Jerusalem. It was the beginning of the struggle for the succession to the throne which dominated the remaining years of David's rule.

The Hebrew people never forgot those years of national glory when David made the nation a power to be respected and feared, from Damascus in the north right to the borders of Egypt. Throughout their history they looked back on this time with pride and longing. When they began to hope for a Messiah, a hero who would rescue them out of their misery, they thought of the Messiah as a second David. And the Messiah's kingdom, the kingdom of God, would resound throughout the world and attract all nations to it.

Betrayal and Reform

THE FIRST AND SECOND BOOKS OF KINGS

Whenever people look back on history, their view is always coloured by their own experiences. They assess and value the events of the past from their own point of view, from the problems of their own times and the solutions which they are seeking.

This is indeed true of the main history books of the Bible. The people who wrote 1 and 2 Kings were able to draw on records of the events they described, and they often refer to them, but they selected from those records, and drew lessons from them, according to their own background. They were men who had seen the Hebrew kingdom and the monarchy collapse in ruins. They had seen the wonderful opportunity left to the nation by King David and his son Solomon betrayed by their successors and the people whom they ruled.

Reform

The main influence on those historians was the period described at the end of the Second Book of Kings, from chapter 22 onwards. Chapter 22 describes the great reform initiated by King Josiah in 622 BC, based on the Book of Deuteronomy. Despite its first blaze of success, that reform failed, and the nation was destroyed by the Babylonians only thirty-four years later in 587 BC. Jerusalem was destroyed and the nation was led away to captivity in Babylon.

Josiah and the religious leaders of his time set out with noble aims. They attempted to purge the nation of all that was unworthy of its position of honour as the children of God and his special people. All pagan practices amongst the Hebrew people were forbidden and the pagan places of worship destroyed. The priesthood was reformed, Jerusalem and its Temple were made the centre of the religion of the whole nation, the central sanctuary where the Covenant would be safeguarded and all the Hebrew people could find their inspiration.

If one wanted a slogan to sum up the whole reform it would be 'one God, one altar, one people'. The whole nation was to be united and purified in the worship and service of God.

A Failed Vision

It was a noble vision, but it failed. When Josiah was killed fourteen years later the whole reform collapsed and the people returned to their old ways. Babylon, a new and more tolerant power, rose to control the Middle East in place of the terrible Assyrians, but the Hebrews were too treacherous to be trusted by any great empire. In the end the Babylonians deported the people of Jerusalem so that they could control the vital frontier with Egypt.

Yet the vision which inspired the reform lived on. When the reformers reflected on their experience, they saw the history of the Hebrew people in a new light. They saw the whole sweep of the nation's development from the entry into Palestine right through to the fall of Jerusalem. The kings were to be judged by their faithfulness to the Covenant. No matter what economical or political success they may have achieved in their times, if they had brought prosperity at the price of the nation's faithfulness to God they were condemned.

It was a very practical approach. If the central principles of the Covenant were forgotten there was little hope for social justice, compassion or fair dealing anywhere in the nation. Might be right.

The Splendour of Solomon

The First Book of Kings opens with all the splendour of

Solomon, son of David, who built on the success of his famous father and extended the wealth and reputation of the Hebrew people. But his reign opened with the murder or suppression of everyone who opposed him, and there are hints throughout it that Solomon's prosperity was based on a ruthless administration and strict control of the nation.

Resentment grew throughout Solomon's reign as he used more and more forced labour for the great fortifications and magnificent buildings he ordered throughout the kingdom. Wealth flowed into the kingdom, and even the Queen of Sheba said that she had no breath left in her when she saw how magnificent it all was. But luxury also brought criticism from Hebrews who longed for the old simple times of the desert fathers.

Solomon left two great memories behind him. The first was enshrined in stone, and became the central symbol of the Hebrew people. This was the Temple which Solomon built at the northern end of Jerusalem to house the sacred Ark. His father, David, had proposed such a building, but it was left to Solomon to realize the project. The seed was sown which would grow into a powerful religious symbol. As the Hebrew religion expanded to meet the needs of the people, so the Temple services grew in magnificence until they eclipsed all other religious centres in Palestine. Indeed, Hebrews throughout the world were to look to the Temple as the source of their inspiration. Yet at the same time Solomon brought in foreign wives and concubines who introduced their native religions. Although Solomon himself remained loyal to the Hebrew religion, the damage had been done.

The other memorial to Solomon is his reputation for wisdom. This is essentially practical wisdom, the political and social sensitivity which marks the successful ruler. Solomon's reputation in this field was so great that the Hebrews attributed all their wisdom literature to him, especially the great collections of proverbs and folk sayings.

Disintegration

However successful Solomon may have been in holding together the many factions in his kingdom, at his death the nation disintegrated. Solomon's son lacked both the potential and the tact of his father. When he tried to bluster, the whole of the northern part of the kingdom, the greater part of the Hebrew people, broke away and formed a kingdom of their own. The nation would never be united again. The two kingdoms, Israel in the north and Judah in the south, became bitter enemies until Israel was destroyed just two hundred and ten years later by the Assyrians. The United Kingdom of David and Solomon had lasted only seventy years. From now onwards the two Books of Kings are the story of the slow decline from the glories of David and Solomon, with only an occasional king who managed to stop the rot for a while.

Despite the failures of the Hebrew kings, both in the northern kingdom and the southern, new witnesses rose who testified fearlessly to the power of God and his Covenant with his people. These were the prophets, who were active throughout the period of the Hebrew monarchy. They fought for the purity of the Hebrew religion and the faith of the ordinary Hebrew, against the pagan religious cults which the leaders so often encouraged. Sometimes these cults endangered the liberty and equality of the ordinary people by giving religious sanction to social divisions, and always there was the degradation of the religious practices associated with the fertility cults. The Canaanite religion was as strong as it had ever been amongst the farmers in the countryside.

Social Justice

In the middle of this period four prophets, Amos, Hosea, Micah and Isaiah, fought for social justice and pleaded with the kings to abandon their international ambitions. Often they pleaded in vain, especially as the growing threat of Assyria was felt in Palestine.

Then came 721 BC, right in the middle of Isaiah's ministry, when the Assyrians destroyed the northern kingdom and marched its people off into an exile from which they never returned. In that terrible disaster the Hebrews of the southern kingdom were actually the allies of the Assyrians in the war against their northern Hebrew brethren. From then onwards for a hundred years, the surviving Hebrew kingdom of Judah was a puppet of the Assyrians.

At the end of the period another great prophet, Jeremiah, attempted once more to bring the nation back to God again. He was associated with King Josiah's great reform, but the national corruption was too deep-seated for Jeremiah to do anything effective. He lived to see his own countrymen in their turn marched away into exile, leaving behind them the ruins of Jerusalem.

Achievements

Yet there were lasting achievements from this period, and we must bear them in mind as we read the Books of Kings. The wonderful stories, from the time of Abraham until the Hebrew people entered Egypt, were written down during this period, as well as the vivid descriptions of the escape from Egypt and the journey through the wilderness. Many of the psalms also belong to these times, and the Hebrew lawyers of the monarchy produced the magnificent collections of laws which have influenced people right down to our own times.

But above all there was the great Temple in Jerusalem. Through the feasts and the services the worship in the Temple helped the Hebrews to apply the Covenant with God to every change in the nation's way of life. Harvest festivals were taken over from the Canaanites, and turned into ways of recognizing the creative power of the God of the Covenant, in the fertility of the land which he had given to them.

When the kingdom finally collapsed and the remaining Hebrew people were marched off into fifty years of Exile in Babylon, they could carry their national life with them. It was enshrined in the writings of the prophets, in the history of their ancestors, in the psalms that they could sing in a foreign land, in the law by which they could live. And when their descendants were at last free to return and rebuild the nation in Palestine again, the traditions of the old Temple in Jerusalem were enshrined in a new Temple which became the centre of the whole of the nation's life.

Traditions such as these were the inspiration of the men who wrote these two books of Hebrew history.

A Priest Looks Back

THE FIRST AND SECOND BOOKS OF CHRONICLES

It is always interesting to have two points of view of something, two different angles on the same events. The author of 1 and 2 Chronicles has just that. His books cover a great sweep of Hebrew history, from King David to the destruction of the kingdom more than 400 years later, which had already been covered by the Books of Samuel and of Kings.

A Priest's View of History
The author of Chronicles is a priest who is looking back on the events from a much later date than the author of the other history books. In fact his work is probably the last to be written in the Old Testament, including the other two books he wrote, both of them history books, the Books of Ezra and Nehemiah. By that time the popular religion of the Hebrew people was centred on the hope for a Messiah and on the great and magnificent services in the Temple in Jerusalem.

The hope for a Messiah was produced by disillusionment with all the efforts of conventional government to make the Covenant with God a reality in the political life of the people. The people's confidence in their kings had been shattered when the kings' policies had led to the destruction of Jerusalem in 587 BC and the people were marched off into exile. Although an effort was made to restore the monarchy when the Exile ended 50 years later, it came to nothing. The new city which rose from the ruins of Jerusalem, and the new nation founded by the determined exiles, was governed by priests. The worship of the Temple in Jerusalem replaced the magnificence of the royal court.

Yet still it seemed that everything went wrong. The people longed to be left free to govern themselves and manage their own affairs, but a succession of great empires fought to control this valuable part of the Middle East. Palestine was a corridor country, with important roads passing through it. The great powers needed to control this area if they were to defend their frontiers and move their armies against their enemies.

There was little hope that the Hebrews, who lived in Palestine, would ever be left free. First the Persians, then Alexander and his Greek soldiers seized control of the area. Although the Hebrews in Palestine were left in peace, and even profited from the trade which flowed through their country, it was far from the promises which they believed that God had given to them. It was an offence to them that the holy land, God's land, should be violated by pagan invaders.

The Longing for a Saviour

When Alexander the Great died the situation was even worse, for his generals fought amongst themselves for the control of his great empire. Palestine became a shuttle-cock which bounced, it seemed, between Egypt and Syria.

The people longed for a deliverer, a saviour who would free the country from its enemies and maintain its borders in peace. Naturally enough they looked back to King David, when the Hebrew empire had been at its greatest, and when a great king ruled in Jerusalem who could repel anyone who dared to attack his kingdom. It mattered little that it was an idealized picture, and that David was only able to rule over a free country because the surrounding great powers were otherwise occupied. No matter how idealized the picture might be, it was an effective symbol in the minds of the people of Palestine. They longed for a Messiah, one anointed with God's power, who would give his people the freedom that they longed for and govern them in God's name.

The Chronicler re-wrote Hebrew history in a way which would support such longings. First he provided lists which showed everyone just where they belonged in the divine scheme. Starting with Adam, the lists trace his descendants all the way down to David, but naturally enough they concentrate on the ancestors of the great king himself.

To the ancient Hebrew, this would be the way of connecting David's authority and power with the authority and power of God himself, at the very beginning of creation. Then there is a detailed history of each of the Hebrew tribes, to show why they are living in the territory that they occupy.

The Temple

The biggest surprise comes early in chapter 6, when the author reaches the lists of officials responsible for the services in the Temple in Jerusalem. He presents them as if David himself had appointed them to their jobs, so that David is made the inspiration for the Temple and its services long before it was built. From then onwards the history shows David as an ideal king without blemishes.

The highlights in his reign are the capture of Jerusalem, the moving of the sacred Covenant Box into Jerusalem, and the Covenant with David and his descendants pronounced by Nathan, the prophet. David duly defeats all the remaining national enemies, and then settles down to plan the building of the Temple. There is no mention of the terrible crime of David, which is given in such detail in the Second Book of Samuel, when he had Uriah murdered so that he could take his wife Bathsheba.

Chapter after chapter is devoted to the planning of the Temple in all its detail, the building of it by David's son Solomon, and its dedication as the religious centre for the whole of the Hebrew people.

Judah and Jerusalem

At the death of Solomon the Hebrew nation split into

two groups, to form northern and southern kingdoms. The southern kingdom, Judah, had as its capital David's city of Jerusalem, so it does not surprise us that this history now confines itself to the kingdom of Judah and its kings. Although the northern kingdom, Israel, was far larger and economically more important than its southern neighbour, the author of this history shows no interest in it. All that matters is whether the kings of David's kingdom are loyal to the law and the Covenant, and whether they support the Temple in Jerusalem. The destruction of the northern kingdom by the Assyrians in 721 BC, surely one of the most dramatic and far-reaching events in the whole of Hebrew history, is not even mentioned.

Naturally enough, King Josiah's reform of Jerusalem and the whole kingdom in 622 BC gets thorough coverage, for this concentrated all Hebrew worship on the Temple in Jerusalem. It is the Temple which is the centre of concern in the brief account of the destruction of Jerusalem and the end of the Hebrew monarchy 35 years later.

Finally, the work ends with the instructions from King Cyrus of Persia that the exiled Hebrews are to be sent back home again, in order to rebuild the Temple. That enlightened worshipper of Zoroaster is given a speech in which he says that it is the Hebrew God who has given him all his power and has ordered him to build the Temple in Jerusalem again. It is a picture which only makes sense if we see it against the background of the times when it was written, and the people for whom this history was intended. They were a people who believed that the worship of God was the most important thing in their lives, and that God was the ruler of the entire universe. They can be forgiven for wanting a history of their people which made these points to the exclusion of everything else. Perhaps this is the way in which people of any generation and any place need their history to be presented to them.

Rebuilding a Nation

THE BOOKS OF EZRA
AND NEHEMIAH

The Books of Ezra and Nehemiah carry the history of the
Hebrews on from the end of their Exile in Babylon. That
Exile ended in 539 BC when King Cyrus of Persia defeated
the Babylonians and gave the Hebrew exiles permission to
return home. He helped them to rebuild Jerusalem, and
the Temple was financed from the Persian treasury, a most
generous act.

High Hopes

It was a time of high hopes, but they soon evaporated.
With the Temple restored, all should have been well with
the Hebrew community in Jerusalem, but they expected
too much. The prophets had promised that God would
come to them in all his glory when Jerusalem was rebuilt
and the new Temple was ready to receive him, but the
expected Messianic age failed to dawn. In fact, the neighbouring peoples succeeded in preventing the Hebrews from
repairing the fortifications of Jerusalem, on the grounds
that the Hebrew people were notoriously rebellious.

The Persian government did a little research and found
plenty of evidence to confirm the Hebrew reputation for
sedition. The walls of the city remained unbuilt. It helps
us to put the Hebrews into their historical perspective
when we realize that Athens was just reaching the height
of its reputation as a city, and it would be another half-
century before the Athenians put Socrates to death.

The denunciations by the prophet Malachi show that
the Hebrew community in Jerusalem was certainly in need
of reform. The priests were neglecting their duty, the
people were failing to support them, and social injustice

was as serious as it had been in the times of Amos and Hosea 200 years earlier. There was a real danger that the small Hebrew community in Jerusalem would disintegrate or at least lose its sense of identity. If it did so there would be little hope that the Jews who had remained behind in Babylon, and Jews living in other cities, would be able to maintain the Hebrew faith. If Jerusalem was lost again, all would be lost.

Two men came to the rescue: Nehemiah and Ezra. The Old Testament puts Ezra first, but it is probable that a later editor has made a mistake about the course of events. It makes more sense if we hold that Ezra followed Nehemiah and completed the work he had begun.

The Official from the Persian Court

Nehemiah was a high official at the court of the Persian emperor. A Hebrew himself, Nehemiah heard about the low morale of the Jerusalem Hebrews and obtained permission to visit the city. He inspected the ruined walls secretly and encouraged the citizens to repair them, backed by written authority from the Persian emperor himself. It was just as well that Nehemiah had such authority, for the local Persian governor did all he could to prevent the work from going on, and in the later stages of the rebuilding the Hebrews had to mount armed guards to protect their workmen.

Nehemiah himself was then appointed governor of Judah, and served for a term of twelve years, during which time he reformed the tax system and gave the people of Jerusalem a sense of security. His measures made Jerusalem an attractive place to many of the Hebrews who had stayed behind in Babylonia, and a stream of new settlers began to arrive. Nehemiah had to return to Persia for a brief period but he was appointed governor again for a further term.

During this second term of office he took strong action to protect the worship in the Temple, and the Jewish sabbath, from neglect and abuse, and he also tackled the problem of marriages to non-Hebrews. There was a real danger that such marriages would sap the Hebrew loyalty to their traditional religion, but Nehemiah did not expect the Hebrews to divorce their foreign wives.

Inspiration

For any lasting reform of the Hebrew community in Jerusalem a more permanent inspiration was needed than any mere administrative reform could possibly provide, and this deeper inspiration was provided by Ezra, who arrived from the Jewish community in Babylon armed with authority over the religious life of all the Hebrews living in the area around Jerusalem.

In this task he was outstandingly successful, thanks to the powerful tool he brought with him. This was no less than 'the Book of the Law of Moses', the opening five books of the Old Testament, or at least a very substantial part of them in the form in which we now know them. These books: Genesis, Exodus, Leviticus, Numbers and Deuteronomy, were given the general title of 'the Law' by the Hebrews. In their historical sections these five books set out the saving acts of God in the creation, the escape from Egypt and the Covenant, all of which give power and meaning to the laws themselves. The law thus becomes the human response to God's saving love, which completes the Covenant between God and man.

So the final editors collected together all the Hebrew laws and placed them alongside the mighty acts of salvation which had been the founding events for the Hebrew people. These laws show the kind of life which God expects from those whom he had saved. The five books were finally written and edited some time towards the end of the Exile in Babylon, and Ezra was the first person to bring them to Jerusalem. Ezra read this great collection of early history and law to the people, while official teachers explained the meaning of it all in the local dialect.

Authority

Backed by such enormously strong authority, Ezra went beyond Nehemiah in the things that he did to protect the purity of the Hebrew faith. In particular, he forced any of the people who had married non-Hebrew women to divorce them and renounce their children. Anyone who did not do this and take the oath within three days had all his property confiscated and was expelled from the Hebrew community. The pattern was set for the exclusiveness of Judaism, with both its strengths and its limitations, which has survived in some places to the present day. Between them Nehemiah and Ezra did much to save the Hebrew community. They preserved its writings for later generations (including our own), and gave the people a sense of identity.

It is interesting to notice that at least one Old Testament author criticized such exclusiveness, in the most delicate way possible. At the very end of the Book of Ruth the author of this little historical romance points out that Ruth the foreigner was the great-grandmother of King David. If David's great-grandmother was a foreigner, what was all the fuss about now?

The Secret Undertaker

TOBIT

One can read this fascinating short story in about twenty
minutes. It seems much more likely to be a parable – Tobit
is the name given to this 'Good Samaritan' – than that it
should have been a factual autobiography. If it were auto-
biographical how odious would the opening lines appear:

> 'I, Tobit, have walked in paths of truth and of good
> works all the days of my life. I have given much in
> alms . . .'

The parable tells of the fortunes and misfortunes of Tobit,
his son, Tobias, and daughter-in-law, Sarah. Tobit took
very seriously the duty of burying the dead – 'I buried,
when I saw them, the bodies of my countrymen thrown
over the walls of Nineveh . . . I also buried those who
were killed by Sennacherib . . . I stole their bodies to bury
them.' He heard of a Jew who had been strangled in the
market place. 'I sprang up at once, left my meal untouched,
took the man from the market place and laid him in one
of my rooms, waiting until sunset to bury him.'

Touches of Humour

The story contains several charming touches of humour.
For example, Sarah, the wife-to-be of Tobias, has an
unfortunate way with her bridegrooms. Her father says to
Tobias, 'My boy, I must be frank with you, I have tried to
find a husband for her seven times . . . and all of them died
the first evening, on going to her room. But for the present,
my boy, eat and drink, the Lord will grant you his grace
and peace.'

After Tobias had gone in to Sarah, her father, somewhat
prematurely, begins to dig a grave. He wants to be able to

bury Tobias without anyone knowing that an eighth suitor of his daughter has perished.

A Book of Prayers

The story is an idyll of happy family relationships, and portrays the virtues of a good Jewish family who might have lived some 200 years before Jesus was born. One notable feature of the book is the number of prayers the author puts into the lips of its dramatis personae. Maybe it is hard to see how Tobit can throw light on our present existence – and that, after all, is what the Bible should do, illuminate the present. Is it perhaps reminding us of the old-fashioned virtue of loyalty, family loyalty, loyalty to the living and respect for the memory of the dead?

Heroic Widow

THE BOOK OF JUDITH

A vast army under General Holofernes is besieging the town of Bethulia. The citizens are on the point of giving in. Judith, 'very beautiful, charming to see', sends for the town elders. 'Listen to me,' she says, 'I intend to do something, the memory of which will be handed down to the children of our race from age to age . . . You must not ask what I intend to do; I will not tell you until I have done it.' (8 : 32-34) Then Judith prays to God to give her courage.

Your strength (Yahweh) does not lie in numbers
nor your might in violent men;
Since you are the God of the humble,
the help of the oppressed,
the support of the weak,
the refuge of the forsaken,
the saviour of the despairing.
Please, please, God of my father . . .
Hear my prayer. . .
And demonstrate to every nation, every tribe
that you are Yahweh, God almighty, all powerful
and that the race of Israel
has you for sole protector. (9 : 11, 12, 14)

She puts on her finery and makes herself beautiful enough to catch the eye of every man who saw her (10 : 4), then leaving the safety of the city she makes her way into the camp of the enemy. Through lies and flattery she gains the confidence of Holofernes. Some days later when he is in a drunken stupor, alone in his tent, she beheads him. Slipping back to Bethulia she encourages the besieged army to make an attack on the enemy. Too late the Assyrians then discover that their general has been assassinated. The whole Assyrian army is completely routed.

Power of God

That briefly is the story of Judith, and not a very edifying one, the reader might be tempted to add. Certainly, one can see clearly enough the moral flaws. But to the Jew before the time of Christ anything was lawful if it protected God's people, especially so if the great power of God was made visible.

The key to the book is to be found in the four lines quoted above :

Demonstrate to every nation, every tribe
that you are Yahweh, God almighty, all powerful
and that the race of Israel
has you for sole protector.

To Encourage the Timid

The Book of Judith dates from about the second century and may well have been written to encourage a people demoralized through the religious harassment of those years. The setting of the 'historical' background is obviously contrived : names, places, peoples are purposefully mixed up. It is as if a writer of today were to say 'Eisenhower led the German troops in the invasion of Britain at the battle of Waterloo. . . .' From this apparently deliberate mix-up we deduce that the preoccupation of the writer was to portray not past Jewish history, but God's present power, and since 'Judith' means 'Jewess', the reliance upon that power of an idealized Jewry.

A Tale of Two Plots

THE BOOK OF ESTHER

Who could ever forget the harrowing pictures of the concentration camps discovered by the liberating armies at the end of World War II? The most tragic scenes of all were surely those showing pathetic lines of Jewish mothers, fathers and children, smiling and waving to the cameras as they walked unwittingly to their death in the gas chambers.

The Book of Esther tells of a plot to massacre Jews, a plot which was not only foiled but was converted into a counter-plot to bring about the death of anti-Semites, a 'pogrom in reverse', as it has been called.

Sinners and Saints

Esther is a well-told short story containing some ironic, if highly improbable, twists and turns. For example, the gallows prepared for the execution of Mordecai the good is used to execute Haman the bad, who had ordered its construction. Like so many Bible happenings, this is not an edifying story and it would not be suitable for reading to youngsters. But then the Bible is as much about sinners as it is about saints.

If it were not for the additions written in Greek and added later, there would be no mention of God in any of Esther's ten chapters. It was included in the Hebrew list of holy books mainly because it appeared to explain the origins of the Jewish Feast of Purim, held in early spring.

Violence Begets Violence

As we read Esther today, we may well recall the persecution of the Jews throughout the ages. While their harassment appears temporarily at an end (except in Soviet Russia), in many countries anti-Semitic prejudices still linger. The moral of this short story from the second or third century BC is valid still: violence always begets violence whether it be against Jew or by Jew. In the long term, love alone can change a situation for the better. Was this the key teaching of the greatest Jew of all?

A Fight for Freedom

THE FIRST AND SECOND BOOKS OF MACCABEES

The Fight for Freedom

The two Books of Maccabees record the very last struggle for freedom fought by the Hebrew people during the Old Testament period. Only twice before, in the reigns of David and Solomon, and of Josiah, had the people been free to govern themselves without interference from foreign occupation troops. Now they were provoked beyond endurance.

This time the foe was the Greek government, which had taken over Palestine at the death of Alexander the Great. Alexander's generals had fought each other for his empire, and it had been parcelled out amongst the antagonists. At first the Hebrews had welcomed the Greek rulers for the Greek culture which they brought with them, but the honeymoon ended abruptly when Antiochus IV declared he was a god. He added the title 'Epiphanes' to his name, to show the divine splendour which he believed shone through him.

The break came when Antiochus plundered the Temple in Jerusalem to pay for a war he was waging against Egypt. Then he paraded his troops outside Jerusalem one sabbath day. While the Hebrews were observing the religious day of rest, the troops occupied the city and established themselves in a stronghold from which they could dominate the inhabitants. Antiochus then set up an altar to the Greek god Zeus in the Temple itself. Immediately a rebellion broke out, led by the Maccabees, a family of country priests.

Help from the Romans

Once more the Greek troops took advantage of the Hebrews' scrupulous observance of the sacred sabbath day. The Greeks attacked the Hebrew army on the sabbath, and the Hebrews refused even to defend themselves. The result was a massacre both of the Hebrew soldiers and of their families.

From then onwards there could be no quarter on either side. At first the rebellion, under the leadership of Judas Maccabaeus, met with considerable success, but Judas himself was then killed and it seemed that all was lost.

Help from a surprising quarter decided the issue, and without violence. By this time, Rome had risen to power and was dominating the Mediterranean world. Hebrew ambassadors met the Roman Senate and entered into an alliance. It is deeply ironical that the Romans, whom the Hebrews so hated a hundred years later, first gained a foothold in Palestine as their allies. Roman diplomacy and intrigue solved the Greek problem for the Hebrews. The Romans supported a rival Greek leader, but only on condition that he was friendly towards the Hebrews. By 150 BC the whole struggle was over. Jonathan Maccabaeus had been appointed high priest and ruler of the Hebrew people, and he was even accepted as a king by the Greek ruler and the king of Egypt.

Two Hebrew religious festivals were instituted to commemorate the struggle for freedom. The Dedication of the Temple keeps alive the memory of the day when the Temple was purified after its defilement by the altar to Zeus, and the Day of Nicanor celebrates the day when Judas Maccabaeus defeated and killed the Greek general of that name.

Why Do You Treat Me So?

THE BOOK OF JOB

'What have I done to deserve this?' Not an easy question
to answer, especially when it comes from one who appears
to have led an exemplary life. This question is implicit
throughout the book of Job. But no answer is given, unless
it is that there is no answer.

From Riches to Rags
The setting of the drama discussion is as follows: Job,
almost certainly an imaginary character, who has led an
upright and honest life, suddenly finds that good fortune
has deserted him. From being a millionaire he becomes a
bankrupt. From being a happy family man he is bereaved
of his children and reviled by his wife. Three friends (and
later a fourth) arrive on the scene ('Job's comforters'). Much
of the book consists of these characters attempting to persuade Job that he must in fact be a sinner and ought to
admit it. This, they claim, would provide a natural explanation for his woes and bring about a reversal of his fortunes.

Looking for a Reason
For the Jews of that time believed that misfortune came
to a person because of an evil life. (Later the Apostles
were to ask Jesus about the man born blind – John 9 : 1 –
'Who sinned, this man or his parents?') One recurring
complaint in the psalms is 'Look how the evil prosper!' –
as though this fact were somehow needing an explanation.
In the Book of Job, the question is reversed: 'Why do
the good sometimes suffer?'

Place of No Return
This problem must have presented the Old Testament Jew

with greater difficulty than the believers in God of later centuries. For up to three or four hundred years before the birth of Christ, Jews were not convinced that there was any life after death, an opportunity for injustices to be righted, virtue rewarded, and evil-doing punished. 'I am going soon and will never come back,' says Job, 'to a land that is dark and gloomy, a land of darkness, shadows and confusion, where the light itself is darkness.' (10:20) And in another place: 'But a man dies, and that is the end of him . . . people die never to rise.' (14:10-12)[1] The believer of today is convinced that all will eventually be made right if not in this life, then in the next. The Jew had no such consolation.

Well-Travelled

The author of this book (written about 500 years before Christ) was evidently a well-travelled person. He speaks of sights and sounds that could not have been experienced in Palestine. In addition he possessed an astonishing literary skill. Much of the Old Testament is written very simply and directly in a way not altogether dissimilar to that in which children write of their experiences. The Book of Job shows a much more sophisticated manner of writing. The dialogues are full of descriptive imagery, the use of similes and metaphors shows that the author was gifted with a highly original imagination.

A Real Relationship

The manner in which Job addresses God might sound shocking to contemporary ears:

No soap can wash away my sins,
Or bleach my hands pure white;
God throws me into a pit with filth,

[1] Some verses later in the book (19:25-26) might seem to argue for a belief in an after-life, but scholars are agreed that these verses are the result of a mistranslation.

And even my clothes are ashamed of me. (9 : 30)
Why, God, did you ever let me be born?
I should have died before anyone saw me.
Isn't my life almost over?
Leave me alone! (10 : 18-21)

But such a manner of addressing God indicates the depth of the intimate relationship that exists between the Jew and God – a relationship that can allow for exasperation, even anger at times. Yet despite the intimacy, there is also the realization that God is wholly the 'Other', the transcendent. 'If God were human, I could answer him; we could go to court to decide our quarrel.' (9 : 32)

Waiting for God

The inconclusive argument between Job and his friends occupies the greater part of the book. Only at the very end does God himself appear on the stage. 'Then out of the storm, the Lord spoke to Job . . .' (38 : 1) It's a magnificent answer. Not because it solves the problem of pain, but rather because it demands of the creature an unconditional belief that the Creator knows what he's doing.

'Where were you when I made the world?' says God to
    Job . . .
'Who decided how large it would be?
Who stretched the measuring line over it? . . .
Have you ever in all your life commanded a day to
    dawn,
Have you ordered the dawn to seize the earth
And shake the wicked from their hiding places?
Have you been to the springs in the depths of the sea,
Have you walked on the floor of the ocean?
Has anyone ever shown you the gates that guard
    the dark world of the dead?
Have you any idea how big the world is?
Answer me if you know.' (38 : 4, 12, 16-18)

So Few Friends

The legend has it that when Teresa of Avila was thrown from her coach into a morass of mud she exclaimed, 'Why do you treat me like this Lord?' A voice was heard to say 'I always treat my friends in this fashion'. 'Then, Lord,' Teresa replied, 'it's small wonder you have so few friends.' This Christian response to suffering, albeit somewhat light-hearted on the surface, is not very far removed from Job's great prayer of trust:

'I was born with nothing, and I will die with nothing.
The Lord gave, and now he has taken away.
May his name be praised!' (1:21)

How to Read Job

The book is not an easy one. Obviously it would be best to read straight through it from beginning to end, but if you think this would present too much difficulty, you may care to do it this way:

The scene	Chapters 1-2
Job's lament	Chapter 3
Eliphaz's comment	4:1-5
	5:8-16
Bildad's comment	8:1-7
Job's reply	10:1-7
Zophar's comment	11:13-15
Job's later comment	27:1-6
Elihu's comment	35:1-12
Yahweh's reply	38
Job's response	42

THE BOOK OF PSALMS

Who finds it easy to pray? So often worries and emotions seem to push out of a person's mind the pious thoughts which many people regard as necessary for prayer. The Jew was not of this opinion. He brought into his prayers just whatever was preoccupying him, for he made little distinction between the sacred and the secular. Everything was God's; everything revealed him; everything could praise him.

> Praise the Lord from the earth,
> sea-monsters and all the ocean depths;
> lightning and hail, snow and clouds,
> strong winds that obey his command.
> Praise him, hills and mountains,
> fruit trees and forests;
> all animals, tame and wild,
> reptiles and birds . . .
> Let them all praise the name of the Lord. (Psalm 148)

Public and Private

The psalms are part poetry, part prayer, part hymn. There are 150 of them collected together in our Bible. At one time it was thought that King David was the author of most of them but now it is recognized that he may have composed only a small proportion. Some of the psalms are meant to be accompanied by musical instruments, and are obviously intended to be recited at public ceremonies.

> All you that are righteous,
> shout for joy for what the Lord has done;
> praise him all you that obey him.
> Give thanks to the Lord with harps,

sing to him with stringed instruments.
Sing a new song to him,
    play the harp with skill, and shout for joy! (Psalm 33)
Other psalms are obviously intended for private use and
reflect a particular need.
    How much longer will you forget me, Lord? For ever?
    How much longer will you hide yourself from me?
    How long must I endure trouble?
    How long will sorrow fill my heart day and night?
    How long will my enemies triumph over me?
    Look at me, O Lord my God, and answer me. (Psalm 13)

Prayers for Today

The psalms are timeless. The believer of today, whether
Christian or not, can make the sentiments of most of
them his own quite as much as the Jew living in 500 BC
evidently did. I say 'most of them' because a few psalms
reflect something of the harsh code that governed the
conduct of war in ancient days.
    Babylon, you will be destroyed.
    Happy is the man who pays you back for what you
    have done to us – who takes your babies, and smashes
    them against a rock. (Psalm 137 : 8-9)
A small number of the psalms contain this sort of venge-
ful prayer and no matter what the interpretation, anyone
living in our society (not much less cruel than the primitive
society of 2000 years ago) would find it difficult to make
such sentiments his own.
    In the main, however, the psalms can be read and
savoured and made completely one's own. They do of
course reflect something of the rural setting in which
they were composed, but even that can be something of a
relief for urban man. As we hear the siren of police car
and fire engine, the roar of traffic, the ceaseless clatter of
countless feet, the verses of the most famous psalm of
all can bring its own quiet peace :

The Lord is my shepherd;
I have everything I need.
He lets me rest in fields of green grass
And leads me to quiet pools of fresh water.
He gives me new strength.
He guides me in the right paths,
As he has promised.
Even though I go through the deepest darkness,
I will not be afraid, Lord, for you are with me.
Your shepherd's rod and staff
protect me.
You prepare a banquet for me,
where all my enemies can see me;
you welcome me as an honoured guest
and fill my cup to the brim.
I know that your goodness and love
will be with me all my life;
And your house will be my home
as long as I live. (Psalm 23)

How to Read the Psalms

Quite briefly, read them as reflective prayers. Decide what particular sort of prayer you would like to express and then choose the appropriate psalm. Here is a short guide:

Psalms of trust	23, 27, 56
Psalms of petition	17, 28
Psalms in time of anxiety	31, 38
Psalms of thanks	30, 116, 136
Psalms of sorrow for sin	51, 130
Psalms of praise	148, 150

THE BOOK OF PROVERBS

'A stitch in time saves nine', 'Too many cooks spoil the broth', 'A rolling stone gathers no moss'. One can only speculate as to the authorship of many of our English-language proverbs. So too with the Book of Proverbs.

The book consists of six different collections of sayings (chapters 1-9; 10-22; 22-24; 25-29; 30; 31), many of them attributed to King Solomon. Certainly he may well have been the author of some; he is, after all, credited with composing three thousand proverbs and over a thousand songs (1 Kings 5 : 12). But it is more likely that most of the proverbs were drawn from further afield.

Skill in Living

Much of the Old Testament is concerned with large issues : the life of the nation, the unity of the people, the worship of God. Proverbs is concerned more with the individual and his skill in daily living. Many of the proverbs appeal to enlightened self-interest. 'If you want to live in harmony and gain the good opinion of people, this is the mentality you must have. . . .'

This may seem to be a long way from the Gospel message 'Blessed are you when men revile you and say all manner of evil things about you. . . .'

'The one who wishes to save his life must lose it . . .'

But self-love (properly understood) and self-respect are the first step on the road to self-sacrifice.

We must also remember that the people who composed and listened to those proverbs were still unaware that a glorious existence beyond the grave was a possibility. All they could glory in for sure was their present existence. And even though the advice offered in the proverbs may appear to be concerned with the methodology of living a trouble-free existence, it is an existence lived in the presence of a loving God. Indeed that is the very meaning of the phrase which concludes the first section of the book: 'the fear of the Lord is the beginning of knowledge'. ('Fear of the Lord' was a descriptive phrase meaning 'a relationship with the Lord'.)

Wisdom Personified
This skill in daily living is strangely personified in chapters 7-8.

'Once I was looking out of the window of my house . . .' (7:6)

'At the entrance to the city, beside the gates, she calls: "I appeal to you . . ." ' (8:4)

'I was born before the mountains . . .' (8:25)

It is strange that in a society which regarded women as little more than 'goods and chattels', this so much admired wisdom should be accorded a feminine, and not a masculine, personification.

How to Read the Book
To read Proverbs straight through would be to overtax one's powers of concentration. The repetitiveness of the proverbs and the constant parallelism has an almost hypnotic effect:

Being lazy will make you poor,
but hard work will make you rich.
A sensible man gathers the crops when they are ready;
It is a disgrace to sleep through the time of harvest.
   (10:4-6)
Beauty in a woman without good judgement
is like a gold ring in a pig's snout.
What good people want always results in good;
When the wicked get what they want, everyone is angry.
   (11:22-23)

Instead one might suggest that a chapter from time to time be used as an objective yardstick with which to measure one's own attitudes. Thus, from chapter 12:

> Anyone who loves knowledge wants to be told when he is wrong. It is stupid to hate being corrected.

(Is the pattern of my life undisciplined, haphazard? How do I react to correction?)

> The Lord is pleased with good people,
> but condemns those who plan evil.

(Am I devious? A schemer? A fixer?)

There are some who would say that the last chapter of all is the finest – 'An alphabetic poem on the perfect wife' (31 : 10-31), though whether it would meet with today's campaigners for the 'liberation' of women is another matter.

What's the Point of it All?

THE BOOK OF ECCLESIASTES

Who has not felt from time to time the uselessness of all human endeavour? One looks back on one's life and recalls the petty ambitions, the superficial relationships, the labour for goals of doubtful worth. This is apparently the mood in which Qoheleth (pronounced Co-hell-leth) jotted down his ideas in his notebook:

It is useless, useless . . . life is useless, all useless.
You spend your life working, labouring and what
do you have to show for it? (1 : 2-3)

Jottings of the Preacher

Qoheleth means 'preacher' and is a translation of the word 'Ecclesiastes'. His thoughts were assembled together around 250 BC. It seems fairly certain that the thoughts of Qoheleth were put on paper spasmodically, not during one intensive bout of writing, for they are random thoughts, following no plan or order. Indeed, at times they are contradictory:

I envy those who are dead and gone;
They are better off than those who are still alive,
But better off than either are those who have
never been born, who have never seen the injustice
that goes on in this world. (4 : 2)
A live dog is better off than a dead lion.
Yes, the living know they are going to die,
but the dead know nothing. (9 : 4)

What Comes After Death

It may be difficult for a believer of today, who has always accepted that there is life after death, to put himself in the place of the Jews of this era who believed in a personal and loving God but who still had little conviction of

survival after death. At an earlier period in their history
they saw survival after death in the life of the people to
which they belonged. But Ecclesiastes was written at a
time when individualism counted for more than had the
community previously. Qoheleth had less reason to feel
optimistic about the future than most other authors of the
Bible's books.

A Time for Everything

Where the book of Proverbs offers a fairly cheerful view of
life and its right ordering, Qoheleth sees rather the vanity
of human achievements and the undoubted truth that one
can't really make oneself happy. God gives a certain number
of joys – let's accept these.

> When man eats, drinks and finds happiness in his work,
> this is a gift from God. (3 : 15)

God is. We exist. God alone knows the plan and purpose
of it all. Death will be inevitable.

The passage from this book with which most people
will be familiar is the famous:

> Everything that happens in this world happens at the
> time God chooses.
> He sets the time for birth and the time for death,
> the time for planting
> and the time for pulling up,
> the time for killing
> and the time for healing,
> the time for tearing down,
> and the time for building.
> He sets the time for sorrow
> and the time for joy,
> the time for mourning
> and the time for dancing,
> the time for making love
> and the time for not making love,
> the time for kissing
> and the time for not kissing.

He sets the time for finding
and the time for losing,
the time for saving
and the time for throwing away,
the time for tearing
and the time for mending,
the time for silence
and the time for talk.
He sets the time for love,
and the time for hate,
the time for war,
and the time for peace. (3 : 1-8)

How to Read It

There is also a time for reading Ecclesiastes – certainly not on a sunny spring morning. It would not take long to read its eleven short chapters but it would almost certainly be a mistake to read them at one sitting. Better wait for the right opportunity, a time of reflection perhaps when one is looking back on one's life, and then to savour just a few of Qoheleth's thoughts at a time.

Love Story

SONG OF SONGS

'The Bible can hardly be called an edifying book,' said a friend to me recently. 'You need look no further than the Song of Songs – just sheer eroticism.' It's true that the five love songs of which this book is comprised are overtly erotic; that is, they express explicitly the sexual desire and joy of lovers. But eroticism is not pornography. The Song of Songs exalts sexuality but speaks of it within the context of love. The pornographer knows only of a sexuality that is joyless and loveless.

Husband and Wife
The love of husband and wife is presented more than once in the Old Testament as the symbol of God's love for his people. The poems contained in the Song of Songs have been interpreted in this way. In the New Testament, St Paul was to take up this theme and apply it to the relationship between Christ and his spouse, the Church.

But one does not have to insist on such an interpretation for the poems to be legitimately included within the covers of our Bibles. After all, God is the author of the beauty of human sexuality no less than of the beauty of nature.

How to Read the Book
Mark off the five poems in your Bible:

    1:5 to 2:7
    2:8 to 3:5
    3:6 to 5:1
    5:2 to 6:3
    6:4 to 8:3

Read them first as one would any other piece of good literature. Then read relating the images to the relationship between Christ and his Church.

C.G.N.

F

THE BOOK OF WISDOM

If a survey were carried out among church-goers today as to their motive for trying to live good lives, how many, one wonders, would say that their choice to do good rather than evil was affected by their belief that one day in a future life they might be rewarded for the good they had done and punished for the evil?

Most of the Jews who lived before Christ gave hardly a thought to a life after death. The reason for this lack of belief was that they had no concept of a human being as body and soul. They would say 'I am a body' rather than 'I have a body'. And since they saw clearly enough that at death the body disintegrated, a continued existence after death seemed to them impossible.

Saints and Sinners

Because the idea of a future life played such a small part in their way of thinking, inevitably they looked to material prosperity here and now as the proof of God's favour – his reward for good behaviour. Poverty and sickness were the visible signs of God's displeasure. A poor person must have been a sinful person.

A Step Forward

The Book of Wisdom, written only 50 or 100 years before Jesus was born, marks a big step forward. Alone among all the books of the Old Testament it refers explicitly to a life after death and the reward or punishment men can then expect:

Yet God did make man imperishable.
He made him in the image of his own nature . . .
The souls of the just are in the hands of God.

No torment shall ever touch them.
In the eyes of the unwise, they did appear to die,
their going looked like a disaster,
their leaving us, like annihilation
but they are in peace.
If they experienced punishment as men see it,
their hope was rich with immortality;
slight was their affliction, great will their blessings be ...
But the godless will be duly punished for their reasoning,
for neglecting the virtuous man and deserting the Lord.
(3 : 1-4, 10)

A Greek Concept

Unlike the Jews, the Greeks believed that people possessed spiritual souls which would live on after the body had died. Since the Book of Wisdom was written in Greek (probably by a Greek-speaking Jew living in Alexandria) we need not be too surprised that we find incorporated in it this Grecian belief in the possibility of a continued personal existence after the disintegration of the body.

A Gift from God

Of course, the book is about more than immortality and the reward or punishment men can expect after death. The author's theme is wisdom. He sees wisdom as much more than common sense, more than the skill of living in such a way as to earn the approval of men. He considers wisdom as a gift from God, and therefore something that should be prayed for since it will lead to a moral way of living. In some passages the author sees wisdom personified as a woman :

She is a breath of the power of God,
pure emanation of the glory of the Almighty ... (7 : 25)
She it was I searched for from my youth;
I resolved to have her as my bride,
I fell in love with her beauty ... (8 : 2)

Poetic Sense

The first nine chapters of the book are concerned with the origin and nature of wisdom, and contain some beautiful passages which display the delicate poetic sense of the author, and his skilful use of similes. To take one example : he puts this self-questioning on the lips of the wicked :

Arrogance, what advantage has this brought us?
Wealth and boasting, what have these conferred on us?
All those things have passed like a shadow, passed like a fleeting rumour.
Like a ship that cuts through heaving waves –
leaving no trace to show where it has passed,
no wake from its keel in the waves . . . (5 : 8-10)

The author then comments :

Yes, the hope of the godless is like chaff carried on the wind, like fine spray driven by the gale;
it disperses like smoke before the wind,
goes like the memory of a one-day guest. (5 : 14-15)

Perhaps of less interest to the contemporary reader are the remaining chapters 10 to 19, in which the author demonstrates at some length the part played by wisdom in the history of the chosen race. The author is obviously at pains to inspire the faith and pride of his fellow Jews in their vocation as God's people, despite the irreligious and sophisticated environment in which they found themselves.

THE BOOK OF ECCLESIASTICUS

Happy the husband of a really good wife;
the number of his days will be doubled.
A perfect wife is the joy of her husband,
he will live out the years of his life in peace . . .
A bad wife is a badly fitting ox yoke;
trying to master her is like grasping a scorpion.
A drunken wife will goad anyone to fury,
she makes no effort to hide her degradation.
A modest wife is a boon twice over . . .
Like the lamp shining on the sacred lampstand
is a beautiful face on a well-proportioned body.
Like golden pillars on a silver base
are shapely legs, are firm-set heels.

(26 : 1-2, 7-11, 13, 17-18)

Is the reader surprised to find sentiments such as these in
'The Good Book'? If he is, then he hasn't yet grasped the
fact that the Bible 'is the word of God but *in words of men*',
and men to whom God was revealing himself in the ordinary
everyday events and relationships of life. The authors of
the Bible books did not look at life as a two-tier universe,
the lower floor containing secular things alien to God, and
the sacred occupying the top storey. The whole of life
was for them God's world and everything in it revealed
God and his active saving presence.

Work of a Scribe

'Ecclesiasticus' was the name given to this book because
of its use by the early *Ecclesia* (Church) as a catechism of
moral instruction for adults seeking baptism. It is not included in non-Roman Catholic Bibles (it did not occupy

a place in the original Hebrew list of books) but was declared one of the inspired books by the Council of Trent.
Its author was a scribe, a leisured and well-travelled member
of upper-crust Jerusalem society writing around about the
year 190 BC. He was obviously concerned at the way in
which Greek influence seemed to be whittling away traditional Jewish manners and mores. This may well have
been the main reason why the scribe, Jesus Ben (descended
from) Sira put these somewhat disconnected thoughts together. He calls upon Jewish traditions, Jewish Law, and
Jewish temple worship (he is obviously a very devout temple
worshipper) to support his appeal. This emphasis on
Jewish customs and loyalty should not lead a contemporary
Gentile to think that the book can say nothing to him.

Wisdom from God

For much of the book is concerned with the acquiring of
skills in the practical management of one's life. The message
is clear enough throughout: this wisdom of managing
one's life well comes from God, is rooted in fear (awe)
of the Lord and inevitably leads to happiness. And Ben
Sira is thinking of 'happiness now' not 'happiness after
death'. The author has not yet come to a realization that
there may be continued existence after death. This could
explain why he frequently speaks of the inevitability of
death :

>   In everything you do, remember your end and you will
>   never sin.
>   Remember the last things and stop hating. (7:36)
>   Remember dissolution and death and live by the
>   commandments. (28:6)
>   When you were born, you were born to be accursed.
>   And when you die, that curse will be your portion.
>   (41:9)

How to Read this Book

These maxims for a happy life follow no special order or

grouping, and the book reads easily and interestingly. One section on forgiveness is not unlike the sermon on the mount (28:1-7). Another prayerful section deals with the glory of God as portrayed in nature (42:15-43:33), a beautiful passage reminiscent of parts of the Book of Job.

Chapters 44-50 reveal why this book was used in the instruction of catechumens, for it gives a comprehensive yet poetic overview of God's plan of salvation for men before the coming of Christ.

It is not unknown for readers to start a novel by taking a quick glimpse at the last chapter, and in fact this might be the best way to read Ecclesiasticus. The first twelve verses of the concluding chapter 51 form a magnificent hymn of thanksgiving. Verses 13-20 describe something of the quest for wisdom made by the author, and should serve as a curtain-raiser for the rest of this attractive and 'contemporary' book.

God is Holy – God is Great

THE BOOK OF ISAIAH
Isaiah 1-39

A survey was carried out among a group of VI Formers: 'Have you ever had a religious experience?' was one of the questions. Perhaps a little ambiguous in its wording, it nevertheless evoked a surprising response. Some 75% replied affirmatively. One reply read as follows:

My religious experience took me by surprise. It happened in an aeroplane. I hadn't been praying or even thinking religiously. But all of a sudden I was conscious of the nearness and greatness and awesomeness of God. It was as though I was seeing the face of a familiar friend, but for the first time. I found myself saying 'So this is You' and for a strange reason I was unable to call this 'You' 'God'. 'God' seemed altogether too formal for someone so close to me, even though for the first time I sensed something of the holiness of God.

Holy, Holy, Holy

The religious experience, the vision, that was to colour Isaiah's understanding and proclamation of God was not dissimilar. It happened to him when he was about twenty years of age:

In the year that King Uzziah died, I saw the Lord. He was sitting on his throne high and exalted, and his robe filled the whole Temple. Around him, flaming creatures were standing, each of which had six wings. Each creature covered its face with two wings, and its body with two, and used the other two for flying. They were calling out to each other : 'Holy, holy, holy! The Lord Almighty is holy! His glory fills the world.' I said: 'There is no hope for me! I am doomed because every word that

passes my lips is sinful, and I live among a people whose every word is sinful. And yet, with my own eyes I have seen the King, the Lord Almighty.' Then one of the creatures flew down to me, carrying a burning coal that he had taken from the altar with a pair of tongs. He touched my lips with the burning coal and said:
'This has touched your lips, and now your guilt is gone and your sins are forgiven.'
Then I heard the Lord say:
'Whom shall I send? Who will be our messenger?' I answered, 'I will go, send me.' (6 : 1-9)

Isaiah, counsellor to kings, taught and wrote in the capital of the southern kingdom, Jerusalem, between the years 740-700 BC. His contemporary in the northern kingdom was Amos. (See page 197)

To understand something of his utterances (collected and edited, but not unfortunately in sequence, by one of his disciples), once again we have to look briefly at the violent history of his time.

Nation of Warriors

Assyria was the power in the land. It was a nation of warriors. Their leader Tiglath-Pileser was an empire builder who had made Syria and the northern kingdom (Israel) his vassals. These two nations made an alliance to overthrow the Assyrian yoke, but they realized that if they were to be successful they would need the support of the southern kingdom, Judah. They marched on Jerusalem to force King Ahaz to join them. 'Then he and all his people were so terrified that they trembled like trees shaking in the wind.' (7 : 2), Ahaz was a weak, unprincipled man. Isaiah, speaking as God's prophet, told him that all he needed to do was to resist passively and the siege would come to nothing; he must put his trust in God, who is 'God with us', 'Immanuel'. (7 : 14)

But Ahaz preferred to trust in Assyria. Isaiah warned him that an appeal for help to Tiglath-Pileser would result in subservience to Assyria. And so it was. Assyria completely destroyed the northern kingdom and exiled its people. And in return, Ahaz found himself, as king of the southern kingdom, not only paying protection money to the Assyrians but even erecting altars in the Temple area to Assyrian gods.

Second Siege

Some years later, the southern kingdom tried to throw off this yoke. An attempt was made to form an alliance against Assyria. Retribution was swift and in 701 Jerusalem was again under siege. Isaiah found himself offering the same advice – 'Only trust in God, and the enemy will disappear'. In 2 Kings 19 one can read how some sort of plague swept through the besieging army and the Assyrians withdrew. Jerusalem was spared. Isaiah's counselling had been proved right.

Empty Sacrifice

Isaiah was concerned with much more than the manoeuvrings of the southern kingdom's 'Foreign Affairs Department'. For some years before his birth the two kingdoms, north and south, had enjoyed a period of great prosperity, but the wealth that had accumulated was not shared among the people. There was much injustice. Many of Isaiah's contemporaries believed that religion demanded no more than an empty ritualistic offering of sacrifice, and this, said Isaiah, was detestable in God's sight:

Do you think I want all those sacrifices you keep offer-
    ing to me?
I have had more than enough of the sheep you burn . . .
It's useless to bring your offerings,
I am disgusted with the smell of the incense . . .
Stop all this evil that I see you doing.
Learn to do right.
See that justice is done –
Help the oppressed,

Give orphans their rights
   and defend widows,
The Lord says, 'Now let's settle the matter.
You are stained red with sin but I will wash you as
   clean as snow.
Although your stains are deep red you will be as white
   as wool.
If you will only obey me,
You will eat the good things the land produces.
But if you defy me
You are doomed to die.' (1 : 11-13, 16-20)

Constant Message

'If you turn away from God, if you trust in men and not
in God, you will bring ruin on yourselves.' Such was the
constant message of all the prophets, and this gloomy prog-
nostication was constantly fulfilled. But throughout it all
there was a message of hope : out of death, God will bring
life. Isaiah's first-born was given the name 'Shear Jashub',
'a remnant shall return' – a symbol of the hope that eventually everything would be righted by God. A day would
come in which justice would prevail because of God's
new chosen leader :
   'A new King will arise from among David's descendants.
   The spirit of the Lord will give him wisdom
   and the knowledge and the skill to rule his people.
   He will know the Lord's will, have reverence for him . . .
   He will not judge by appearance or hearsay; he will
   judge the poor fairly and defend the rights of the
     helpless.' (11 : 1-4)
The Christian sees these words verified in the person of
Jesus Christ.

How to Read Isaiah

Chapters 1-39 are a collection of sayings given at various
times to meet differing situations, and they are not in
chronological order. Rather than attempt to read the book

through from beginning to end, it might be better to study a few passages, and the following selections are suggested:

The prophet's vision	6:1-11
Immanuel – God is with us	7:14-23
A Messiah will come to save us	2:2-4, 9:1-7
Social Injustice	3:14-24
The Remnant	4:2-6
The Song of the Vineyard	5:1-7
The Golden Age to Come	11:1-16
A Song of Thanksgiving	12:1-6

A Second Isaiah

Chapters 40-66 of the book were included under the authorship of Isaiah because of an accident of editing. They are, in fact, the work of one (or possibly two) author(s) who lived some two hundred years later. These writings will be discussed in the following chapter.

Cry Holy

The first Isaiah has been described as the prophet of God's holiness. But what is holiness? It's an elusive enough quality to define when we are speaking of a human being, but to describe God as 'holy' – this is even more elusive of definition.

The basic meaning of the word 'holy' is 'separateness', 'otherness'. When a man is aware of the total otherness of God he becomes filled with an awesome fear which repels ('Depart from me, Lord,' said Peter after he had caught a glimpse of the holiness of Jesus), and at the same time attracts. Many of our religious ideas demand that we keep a correct balance between 'opposites'. The otherness (transcendence) of God and his nearness (immanence) is but one example.

Isaiah adored and proclaimed the utter holiness, the otherness, of God, yet declared too that this God is for ever with us: 'Immanuel'.

THE BOOK OF ISAIAH
Isaiah 40-66

Who could ever forget the plight of the Jews in Nazi Germany? One recalls in particular those harrowing and heart-rending films of Jewish family groups with pathetically small bundles of belongings being herded on to trains bound for camps at Auschwitz and Dachau and Belsen. Anyone with a knowledge of the Old Testament would have recognized in those scenes history repeating itself.

After the total destruction of Jerusalem in 587 by the Babylonian army, the inhabitants of the city were herded together a few miles away in a village called Ramah. Some few were executed, some pardoned, some allowed to remain among the ruins, but the vast majority were deported to Babylon, 500 miles eastward, exiles for the next 49 years.

A Better Fate

Most of these exiles were to meet with more mercy than the victims of the Nazis. They were allowed to settle in their new country, own their property, cultivate the land. Of course, those with a deeper sense of national identity longed for the city from which they had been banished:

> By the rivers of Babylon
> We sat down, there we wept when we remembered Zion.
> On the willows nearby we hung up our harps.
> Those who captured us told us to sing;
> They told us to entertain them:
> 'Sing us a song about Zion!'
> How can we sing a song to the Lord in a foreign land?
> May I never be able to play the harp again, if I forget
> you, Jerusalem . . . (Psalm 137)

Some felt that their own God had abandoned them. The

truth was rather that they had abandoned their God, and as all the prophets had warned, they had brought ruin on themselves. All the glory of the nation, painstakingly built up over five hundred years from the time of David and Solomon, was ended. Certainly many of them were tempted to join in the colourful Babylonian rituals whose more human gods were more manageable and malleable (literally) than their own.

Fellow Exiles

It was to his fellow exiles that the writer of the Book of Isaiah (chapters 40-55) wrote this collection of consoling poems. Although included in the Book of Isaiah, chapters 40-55 were written by an anonymous poet-prophet some two hundred years after the Jerusalem Isaiah (see previous chapter). For the sake of convenience, he is given the title 'Deutero [second] Isaiah', or 'Babylon Isaiah'. We know nothing about his life. We know him only by his poetry as a most sensitive writer, with a breath-takingly vast view of the greatness of God:

To whom can the holy God be compared?
Is there anyone else like him?
Look up at the sky.
Who created the stars you see?
The one who leads them out like an army,
he knows how many there are and
calls each one by name!
His power is so great —
not one of them is ever missing! (40:25-26)

This God is the creator and redeemer of all men, and he is present now to his people in the pagan land of Babylon, and wanting their happiness.

God's Anointed

The cause of Deutero-Isaiah's hope was a pagan, Cyrus the Great. From a humble principality he had risen to create and dominate an empire that stretched from Egypt to India. Even before he threatened Babylon he was foreseen by the prophet as the liberator of the Hebrew exiles: '

'Comfort my people',
says our God, 'Comfort them!
Encourage the people of Jerusalem.
Tell them they have suffered long enough
and their sins are now forgiven.' (40 : 1-2)
The Lord has chosen Cyrus to be king.
He has appointed him to conquer nations;
   he sends him to strip kings of their power;
   the LORD will open the gates of cities for him . . .
I appoint you to help my servant Israel,
   the people that I have chosen.
I have given you great honour,
   although you do not know me.
I am the LORD; there is no other god.
   I will give you the strength you need,
   although you do not know me.
I do this so that everyone
   from one end of the world to the other
   may know that I am the LORD
   and that there is no other god. (45 : 1, 4-6)

It All Happened

Babylon was declared an open city to Cyrus and his troops. One of the victor's first acts was to return the Temple vessels (confiscated fifty years previously by the Babylonians) to the Jews and tell them they were free to go. Not all of them were anxious to leave. Many had no nostalgia for Jerusalem. They knew that it was a city in ruins, that the surrounding farm lands were either occupied by squatters or else overgrown with weeds. To inspire these reluctant repatriates with enthusiasm the Babylon Isaiah compared the future return of the exiles to Jerusalem to that glorious Hebrew epic: the escape from slavery in Egypt across the desert to the promised land. (41 : 17-20)

Suffering Servant

We need to look on the contents of those chapters as a miscellany of poems devoted to a number of subjects: the choice of Cyrus as the agent of God, the glorious return to Jerusalem, the greatness of the saving God, the folly of worshipping man-made gods. There are also at least four poems devoted to the Suffering Servant ('servant' might be better translated as 'slave'). These are:

The choice of the servant	42:1-4
The servant's calling	49:1-7
The servant's confession	50:4-9
The atoning death of the innocent servant	52:13-53:12

Who is this servant? Is it the nation? Is it an individual? Is it a Jewish saint from the past or a contemporary of the prophets? Or could it be a combination of individual and nation? These questions have long puzzled scholars and may never be answered. However, no Christian can read those passages without immediately referring them to Jesus, the Christ. Indeed, we know that Jesus was familiar with this Book of Isaiah (see Luke 4:16-20) and it may well be that in meditating on those four poems he saw his own destiny.

The Return Home

The returned Jews indeed discovered that life back in their homeland was bitter and hard, and the remaining chapters of the Book of Isaiah (chapters 56-66) seem to reflect something of this disillusionment. Many scholars say that these chapters are the work of two post-exilic authors. They are faithful to the teaching of the two previous 'Isaiah's', there are many references to guilt and its expiation.

Correct Order

It is worth keeping in mind that the Books of Isaiah, Jeremiah (Lamentations), Baruch, and Ezekiel were not printed in our Bibles in a correct chronological order, and should be edited as follows:

Isaiah, 1-39
Jeremiah
Lamentations
Ezekiel
Isaiah, 40-55
Isaiah, 56-66

How to Read Deutero-Isaiah

One method would be to pick the subjects and read individual passages rather than all the chapters in sequence. So:

Cyrus is God's instrument of liberation	41:1-7
God is with his people	41:8-16
The Majesty of God	40:12-26
First Servant Song	42:1-4
A Liberation like Exodus	42:10-16
The false Babylonian Gods – a satire	44:9-20
Second Servant Song	49:1-7
Third Song	50:4-9
Fourth Song	52:13-53:12

Deutero-Isaiah marks the high point of Old Testament literature and theology. In these chapters we are given an exalted vision of God and his saving love for all men. It surpasses that of any other Old Testament book. Jesus's choice of this book as the source of the text for his first sermon in his home town leads one to believe that this opinion would have been shared by him too.

THE BOOK OF JEREMIAH

The Bible is mainly about people – good people, bad people, and people who were a mixture of good and bad. It is thus a fairly true reflection of our contemporary world.

Of all the many characters who appear throughout the pages of the Bible, perhaps the most tragic of all is Jeremiah. This is not to say that he was a sad man – a popular misconception. Rather he was a person constantly at odds with the aims of the society in which he lived because he realized that those aims were leading away from God towards self-destruction. Much of his life story is bound up with the turbulent and swiftly-changing history of his age. The three great power blocs were, at one time or another during this period, the Assyrians, the Babylonians, and the Egyptians. Their varying relationships with the southern Jewish kingdom (Judah) form the changing back-cloth to much of Jeremiah's message. To have a complete understanding of that message one would need to dis-entangle the complicated series of alliances and aggressions between the four nations. Such would be outside the scope of a work such as this.[1]

However, one can glean something of the historical back-ground by reading 2 Kings, chapters 22-25 and the Book of Jeremiah, chapters 40-44.

Life Story

Jeremiah was a reluctant prophet. At about twenty years of age he received his call:

The Lord said to me, 'I chose you before I gave you

[1] Readers looking for a more detailed historical treatment of the time are advised to study such works as *The Prophets and the Law* by Joseph Rhymer or Anderson's *The Living World of the Old Testament.*

life, and before you were born I selected you to be a
prophet to the nations.'
I answered, 'Sovereign Lord, I don't know how to speak;
I am too young.' (1 : 4-6)

Later on in his 'career' as prophet, Jeremiah was to speak
bitterly to God:

Lord, you have deceived me, and I was deceived.
You are stronger than I am and you have overpowered
me.
Everyone makes fun of me; they laugh at me all day long.
Whenever I speak, I have to cry out, and shout,
'Violence! Destruction!' Lord, I am ridiculed and
scorned all the time because I proclaim your message.
(20 : 7)

Good King Josiah

Not long after Jeremiah's call, Josiah became king. The
religious state of the nation was disastrous. (It is described
by Jeremiah in chapters 2 and 3.) The practice of black
magic, human sacrifice, 'sacred' prostitution, was rife.
Josiah's desire for a reformation coincided with the 'discovery' of at least part of the Book of Deuteronomy hidden
in the Temple walls. When the king read this document, he
realized just how far from God's way the nation had strayed.
He immediately undertook a massive programme of reform: he repudiated the worship of idols, he insisted on
the celebration of traditional Jewish festivals, and, to
prevent abuses, he made it unlawful to offer sacrifice anywhere but in Jerusalem itself. Jeremiah's priest-father at
Anathoth (a few miles away from Jerusalem), was one
among many whose priestly calling was endangered by this
decree. In openly backing up Josiah's reform (11 : 1-8)
Jeremiah incurred the anger of his own kinsfolk (11 : 18-23).
This hurtful antagonism was the first of the many agonizing
misunderstandings which were to earn Jeremiah the opprob-
rium of all sections of society.

The Reform Fails

Despite all King Josiah's efforts, it seemed that the reform he had instituted could not inspire the people. Jeremiah tried to stir his fellow countrymen to reform by pointing to the barbarous threat from the north – the Scythians. These were undisciplined nomads from Russia who pillaged and murdered; anarchic guerrillas without a cause. (See chapters 4-6) But his prophecies had little effect. (In fact the threat of the Scythians never materialized.)

After Josiah was killed in battle, his successor was a useless puppet of the Egyptians and all efforts at reform now simply faded away. The history of the people from then onwards was to be one of continued moral decline until Jerusalem was finally destroyed by the Babylonians 22 years later.

The lesson to Jeremiah was plain: until there is a change of heart, reform is impossible. Reform must come from within; it cannot be imposed by laws from without. But can change come 'from within' if there is something basically wrong with man? Jeremiah's answer was to insist that man depends totally on God if he is to change. Jeremiah prayed for the healing power of God to become operative in his life and the lives of the people. (See chapters 30-33 but especially 31 : 31-34)

Attempts on His Life

A first attempt was made on Jeremiah's life by the religious 'establishment' after he had prophesied that God would allow the Temple to be destroyed because of the hypocrisy and complacency of the worshippers. (See chapter 26) In the very Temple precinct Jeremiah had proclaimed 'I will make this house like Shiloh' – Shiloh, once a centre of worship, had been utterly destroyed. Jeremiah escaped only because a group of officials counselled moderation. Even so he was 'excommunicated' from the Temple.

Babylon, by now (698 BC) the most powerful nation, laid siege to Jerusalem and eventually captured the city. It was a comparatively mild sacking; the king and some of his people were taken into captivity in Babylon. Jeremiah foresaw that those who were left behind in the city might mistake the mildness of the Babylonians for softness. He realized that the Babylonian policy of toleration was dictated from a position of strength not weakness. To think otherwise would be a most dangerous miscalculation. To try to forestall this, the prophet acted out various mimes in front of the people : he wore a yoke, first of wood, later of iron, and spoke to the people. 'Thus says God,' Jeremiah proclaimed :

'If any nation will not submit to his rule, then I will punish that nation with war, starvation and disease.'
(27 : 5-8)

Thought to be a Traitor

Despite his preaching, the Jews revolted again and in consequence Babylon laid siege to Jerusalem. This siege lasted for more than two years, and throughout Jeremiah constantly urged the people to surrender. This, naturally enough, was regarded as treason. He was lowered by ropes into a filthy cistern and left to die. Only the loyalty of a friend at court saved him from death. The city fell to the Babylonians. The king was blinded after seeing his sons murdered. Jerusalem was flattened to the ground. All citizens except the very poorest were taken into exile, but Jeremiah stayed behind. He saw in this desolation the hand of God purifying his people. The suffering would not be in vain. There would be a resurrection, but first there must be a dying.

Little is known about Jeremiah's death other than that it was in Egypt, possibly at the hand of fellow Jews.

How to Read the Book

Because the contents of the Book of Jeremiah as printed in our Bibles are not in chronological sequence, it makes for difficult reading. Possibly the best way would be to read selected passages under the following headings:

All is Desolation

THE BOOK OF LAMENTATIONS

The poet wandered sadly among the ruins of the devastated city. Jerusalem, its Temple flattened to the ground, was emptied of its people, now exiled in Babylon. The silence of death lay over the desolate acres. This may well have been the scene which provoked the writing of the five dirges that make up the Book of Lamentations. At one time these poems were ascribed to Jeremiah himself, but scholars now believe that they are the work of another hand (or hands).

Why did our God allow this terrible thing to happen? the poems ask. Not because he was a weak God. Not because he had deserted his people. This devastation was a punishment for the people's constant infidelity, but a punishment that was not vindictive but healing, not leading to despair but to penance and repentance.

In the last poem we have a prayer for mercy:

But you O Lord, are King for ever and will rule to the
    end of time.
Why have you abandoned us so long?
Will you ever remember us again?
Bring us back to you, Lord! Bring us back.
Restore our ancient glory. (5 : 19)

THE BOOK OF BARUCH

For a book to be published under another man's name may seem to us to be highly irregular, but in the centuries immediately preceding the birth of Christ it was so common a practice as to offend or deceive no one.

The authors of this book claimed Jeremiah's secretary as their identity, but in fact they lived much later, probably at the beginning of the second century BC. The book falls naturally into four sections:

A prayer of sorrow	1:13-3:8
The meaning of true wisdom	3:9-4:4
A poem of hope	4:5-5:9
A letter of warning against idol worship	6:1-72

Jeremiah himself is claimed as the author of the latter but one need give no more credence to this than to the supposed authorship of the rest of the book.

THE BOOK OF EZEKIEL

Nebuchadnezzar is the tongue-tripping name of the most famous king of Babylonia. Babylon, the capital, was situated just north of the city we now know as Baghdad, some five hundred miles east of Jerusalem. Nebuchadnezzar stormed and conquered Jerusalem in the year 597 BC. He ordered that the principal citizens be deported to Babylonia, and among the exiles were the priest Ezekiel and his wife.

Pleasant Living

The reader might be forgiven for imagining that exile in Babylon was not much different from a contemporary description of slave-labour-camp life in Russia. That would not be true. The exiles in Babylon were allowed to live normal lives; so normal and free from harassment that there was some danger of their losing their national identity and adopting the grosser forms of idol worship practised by their captors.

If anyone harassed the Jews in exile it was Ezekiel. Five years after settling in Babylonia he received his call to be a prophet – that is, to become the conscience of the people.

. . . I was living with the Jewish exiles by the Chebar River in Babylonia. The sky opened and I saw a vision of God . . . When I saw this, I fell face downwards on the ground, then I heard a voice saying, 'Mortal man, stand up . . . I am sending you to the people of Israel.'

(1 : 1, 27, 2 : 3)

Religious Peril

The religious peril for the Israelites was that they might

argue thus: 'Babylon overcame Jerusalem: therefore the gods of the Babylonians are mightier than the God of the Israelites'. Moreover, in a certain way the god of the people in those ancient days was related locally to the land of the people. If the Israelites had left their land five hundred miles behind them, they were also liable to think that they had left their God also – the God who resided in the Temple at Jerusalem – and that now it was time to worship the gods of their new land. Ezekiel was a stern prophet; he castigated his own people for their fickleness. He insisted that God was not confined to the Temple; that he was everywhere. He insisted on the personal responsibility of the individual for his behaviour. Hitherto the Jews had paid little attention to the individual's morality; this had been almost completely overshadowed by the collective morality of the nation.

Four Sections

The Book of Ezekiel is clearly divided into four sections:

Warnings given by the prophet before the second fall of Jerusalem in 587	1-4
Warnings against neighbouring nations	25-32
Hopeful promises after the fall of Jerusalem	33-39
The new Temple and the new Jerusalem	40-48

The second and fourth sections are difficult, the former because of its bloodthirsty language not inappropriate for its time but alien to our way of thinking now. The fourth section is tiring to read because of the mass of imaginative detail concerning the reconstruction of the Temple.

How to Read the Book

Ezekiel had a vivid imagination. Not only is this clear

from his writings, it is also apparent in the 'mimes' (described in the book) he acted out for the benefit of his contemporaries. Several passages from this book stand out as masterpieces of religious insight. One might suggest the following sections as giving the heart of Ezekiel's message:

Hope for the Future

This vision of the dry bones revived into new life offered to the exiled people a vivid parable of the new life awaiting them.

'Mortal man, the people of Israel are like these bones. They say that they are dried up, without any hope and with no future. So prophesy to my people Israel and tell them that I, the Lord God, am going to open their graves. I am going to take them out and bring them back to the land of Israel. When I open the graves where my people are buried and bring them out, they will know that I am the Lord. I will put my breath in them, bring them back to life, and let them live in their own land. Then they will know that I am the Lord. I have promised that I will do this – and I will. I, the Lord, have spoken.' (37:11-14)

THE BOOK OF DANIEL

In our own times many people have seen their homeland overrun by invaders, and their traditional way of life threatened or destroyed. In Biblical times invasion and persecution were frequent experiences for the Hebrew people. Indeed, there was hardly ever a period when foreign troops were not occupying their country and trying to make people abandon their religion.

The Literature of Persecution

Times of persecution produce a special kind of literature, songs of protest and defiance become well-known and popular. The people listen eagerly to stories which give them encouragement and hope. The leaders of the Hebrew people wrote such stories, some of which have been preserved in the Bible, but they knew that open defiance would be punished as rebellion, so the real meanings of their protest songs and stories were hidden carefully. The words seem innocent when taken literally, for the stories are about heroes of another time. But the people who sang the songs and listened to the stories knew that they really referred to their own situation and to their own leaders.

The Book of Daniel is just such a story. It tells of Daniel and three other Hebrew youths who were taken as slaves by a foreign invader to be trained as scribes in the royal court. They were well treated, and their wisdom quickly gained them special privileges and esteem. The inevitable moment arrived when their Hebrew faith was put to the test. Their masters did all in their power, by persuasion and by force, to make them abandon their religion, but God protected them in every danger. Even the foreign king himself was convinced, and decreed that his Hebrew subjects must be left free to practise their religion.

The Setting

The apparent setting for the story is the Exile, when Jerusalem was captured by the Babylonians in 598 BC and the court officials were deported to Babylon with their families. The true situation is more likely to be a little over 400 years later, when Greek and Egyptian kings were fighting for control of Palestine. During a period of Greek control, the Greeks tried to stamp out the traditional Hebrew way of life and imposed Greek culture on the people. At the climax of the persecution, in 167 BC, a statue of Zeus was placed in the Temple in Jerusalem, and sacrifices were offered to the Greek god.

The Hebrews rose in rebellion under the leadership of Judas Maccabaeus, and began a guerrilla war which raged for seven years before the Greeks were finally defeated and forced to withdraw.

The Book of Daniel made stirring reading for people living in such difficult times. Not only does it tell of God's protecting power, but it goes on to prophesy the defeat of every great empire which attempts to dominate the world. God alone is the true ruler of the world, and all history is under his control. One passage in particular, in chapter 7, paints a vivid picture of the final times when the saints of God will be at war with God's enemies. God's army rides upon the clouds. Its leader is a man whom God makes king over all peoples, to rule the final empire of God, which no evil power will ever destroy.

This is the Hebrew hope for a Messiah, which was first expressed by Isaiah more than 500 years earlier, during another period when the Hebrews were threatened by foreign attack.

The Book of Daniel contains the last of the Old Testament prophecies of a Messiah, and some of the most powerful poems of faith and hope to be found anywhere in the Bible.

Love Story

THE BOOK OF HOSEA

In our contemporary society and culture the unfortunate partner of a broken marriage would say: 'My marriage has broken down. I suppose there may have been faults on both sides, but I believe we were badly matched.' The Jew of ancient days spoke as though it was God's plan for the marriage to fail. As we have seen elsewhere (page 34), the Bible writers and editors attributed every happening, good and evil, immediately to God; they ignored secondary causes. And so the Book of Hosea begins thus:

> When the Lord first spoke to Israel
> through Hosea, he said to him,
> 'Go and get married; your wife
> will be unfaithful, and your
> children will be as bad as she is.' (1:2)

Come Back to Me

Hosea married Gomer and there were three children. Whether Hosea was the father of the second and third children is not clear. What we do know is that before long Gomer had grown tired of Hosea and went after another lover or lovers. According to Jewish law, Hosea could have demanded the death penalty for Gomer, he could have had her stoned to death. (See the Gospel of John, chapter 8:3) Instead, he took the comparatively lenient course of divorcing her. But he could not forget his love for Gomer. He sought her out and when he had found her, he took her back, and he tried to regain her affection for himself.

Lesson of Experience

We tend to divide our world into two: the sacred and

the secular; the sacred is God's province, the secular is
ours. This dichotomy is of our making, not God's. His
world is one world and he loves it all because he made
it. The Jew of Biblical times thought of the world as one:
all of it was sacred because it all revealed God and his
desire to save men. So it was with Hosea as he contemplated
the patched-up wreckage of his marriage. 'This is how
God treats his people,' he thought. 'My marriage has been
a mess, but where else have I got my willingness to forgive
Gomer and love her again but from God? His people,
my people, since they left the desert in their escape from
slavery in Egypt have constantly been unfaithful to the
God who loved and saved them. That time in the desert
was a honeymoon – the time of love between God and his
people away from all other enticements. But since then,
just as Gomer played the harlot with me, so have my
fellow countrymen with God. And just as I have forgiven
Gomer, so God is ready to forgive his spouse, Israel, provided she will turn back to him.'

> So I am going to take her into the desert again; there I
> will win her back with words of love . . . She will respond
> to me there as she did when she was young, when she
> escaped from Egypt. Then once again she will call me
> her husband – she will no longer call me her Baal . . .
>
> (2 : 14-17)

Hosea contrasts the faithless turning away of his people
with God's steadfast love (in Hebrew – Hesed).

> Israel, I will make you my wife
> I will be true and faithful
> I will show you constant love and mercy
> and make you mine forever. (2 : 19)

Priests are to Blame

Hosea was preaching in the north at about the same time
as Amos, that is, in the middle of the eighth century BC. He
castigated the priests for the irreligious state of Israel:

> The Lord says,

'Let no one accuse the people or reprimand
them – my complaint is against you priests.
Night and day you blunder on, and the prophets
do no better than you ...
You priests have refused to acknowledge me
and have rejected my teaching, and so I reject
you and your sons as my priests.' (4 : 5-6)

Mercy not Sacrifice

The priests did nothing to discourage the people's belief
that the offering of sacrifice automatically pleased God.
They should rather have been preaching that sacrifice must
be preceded by a change of heart. They may have neglected
this corrective preaching because they were hardly convinced of it themselves, or else because they realized that
their living would suffer if the number of sacrifices
dwindled :
The Lord says :
'What I want from you is plain and clear :
I want your constant love (Hesed)
not your animal sacrifices. I would
rather have my people know me
than burn offerings to me.'
('Know me' means 'have a relationship of love
with me')
Jesus, some 700 years later, was to quote from this passage
twice. (Matt. 9 : 13, 12 : 7)

Love of a Father

In chapter 11 Hosea, reflecting perhaps on his compassion
for his own children, changes the metaphor from the love
of a bridegroom for his bride to that of a father for his
baby child :
Yet I was the one who taught Israel to walk.
I took my people up in my arms
but they did not acknowledge that I
took care of them.

I drew them to me with affection and love.
I picked them up and held them to my cheek;
I bent down to them and fed them . . .
How could I give you up, Israel?
How could I abandon you?
Could I destroy you as I did Admah?
Or treat you as I did Zeboiim?
My heart will not let me do it!
My love for you is too strong. (11 : 3-4, 8)

Whereas Amos simply described the wrath of God as inevitable and inexorable, Hosea saw God's anger as redemptive. God does not want the death of a sinner. His love is liberating not destructive.

How to Read Hosea

The invective and the denunciation found in many of the Old Testament prophets, including Hosea, may make little appeal to the reader of today but there is also much of tenderness and compassion. Read especially chapter 2 : 1-23 and chapter 11 and you will see how unfair it is to describe the God of the Old Testament simply as a God of wrath.

A New Spirit

THE BOOK OF JOEL

An Archbishop confessed : 'I had half an hour to spare and I went into my chapel. I was not really in a praying mood. I said : "Well, Lord, here I am. I don't know quite how I'm going to occupy the next thirty minutes but I hand myself over to you. I hold nothing back. Do with me what you want." No sooner had I said these words than I was aware that the Spirit of God had taken hold of me. I experienced a sense of utter joy and complete peace quite beyond anything I had ever known before. It came as something of a prosaic surprise to me to find myself carving the Sunday joint half an hour or so later.'

Open to All
This Archbishop now holds weekly prayer meetings in his house. The meetings are open to everyone and comprise members of almost every denomination. At these meetings several people 'speak in tongues' – including the Archbishop himself. These demonstrations of the presence of the Spirit are not brash exercises in exhibitionism. One hardly notices them as they pray, and the ability to 'speak in tongues' seems to take the speakers as much by surprise as everyone who witnesses them.

Outpourings
These outpourings of the Spirit are seemingly more frequently witnessed now than at any time since the early days of the Church. The great coming of the Spirit at Pentecost was, of course, the one referred to by St Peter. The effect of the Spirit on himself and the other Apostles had led people to believe they were all drunk. He modestly denies the allegation. 'After all,' he said, 'it's only 9 o'clock

in the morning.' (Acts 2:15) And then he goes on to quote
from the Book of Joel:

In the days to come – it is the Lord who speaks –
I will pour out my spirit on all mankind.
Their sons and daughters shall prophesy,
Your young men shall see visions,
Your old men shall dream dreams.
Even on my slaves, men and women,
in those days, I will pour out my Spirit.
I will display portents in heaven above
and signs on earth below.
The sun will be turned into darkness
and the moon into blood
before the great day of the Lord dawns.
All who call on the name of the Lord will be saved.

(3:1-5)

This passage could well be regarded as the heart of the
Book of Joel.

The Heart of the Book

Nothing is known about Joel, even the date of his prophecy
is a matter of speculation. Some scholars have suggested
600 BC – others have put it as late as 350 BC.

The cause of his prophecy seems to have been an extra-
ordinarily severe plague of locusts. As we have seen elsewhere, the Jews saw God very actively present in all the
happenings of their world. Not for them a God who was
imprisoned in his heaven! And so too in this devastating
plague Joel sensed that God was speaking through him
(Joel) to his people. He saw in this event a vivid presenti-
ment of the *Day of the Lord* – a day of wrath and cosmic
convulsion, a final judgement of mankind. Whereas in
other prophets such as Amos this day would be one of un-
relieved doom, in Joel there is more than a hint of hope.
'Israel,' he seems to say, 'will be vindicated in this judgement.'

To the urban dweller of today, a plague of locusts may evoke hardly a tremor of terror. If Joel were alive today he might regard a total break in electricity supplies, or the paralysis through industrial action of a whole great city, a catastrophe equivalent to a plague of locusts.

The message is the same whether for 500 BC or AD 1980: the Day of the Lord is surely coming and we shall all one day be accountable for the way we have responded to God's prompting Spirit.

THE BOOK OF AMOS

If you stand on the balcony at the back of the souvenir shops on the road from Nazareth to Jerusalem, you find yourself looking out on a desolate and deserted area called the 'wilderness of Judea'. The view won't do justice to your colour camera, for the scenery for mile upon mile is a mixture of grey and brown – grey limestone outcrops, and sparse grass burnt brown by sun and lack of water.

It was in this wilderness that Amos, the first writing prophet of the Old Testament, lived the utterly frugal life of shepherd and farm labourer. He was not a 'professional' prophet:

'I am not the kind of prophet who prophesies for pay,' he said. 'I am a herdsman and I take care of fig trees. But the Lord took me from my work as a shepherd and ordered me to go and prophesy to his people, Israel.'

(7:14-16)

Seer of Visions

In the solitude of the wilderness, Amos reflected on the journeys he had made taking his produce to markets in the north. It was about the year 750 BC and the land was at peace. There should have been prosperity for everyone. But in his travels Amos, simple countryman though he was, saw little but injustice and corruption. The gulf between the rich and the poor was wide indeed. The rich believed that their wealth was a sign of the Lord's pleasure at their correct performance of rituals and sacrifice. If the poor were poor, they argued, this was a mark of God's displeasure, something to be expected: the peasants, after all, seemed uninterested in temple worship.

A Pair of Sandals

Amos had noticed too that the peasants were unable to secure justice. When their crop failed, the rich lent them money at exorbitant rates of interest. If the poor then went to court, bribery would soon see that the verdict went against them. 'We'll find a poor man who can't pay his debts, not even the price of a pair of sandals, and buy him as a slave.' (8:6) It may have been while he was reflecting in the stillness of the countryside on all this rottenness that Amos had the visions he was later to describe: a vision of locusts (7:1-3), a subterranean fire (7:4-6), a plumb line:

> I had a vision from the Lord. In it I saw him standing beside a wall that had been built with the use of a plumb line . . . 'I am using it' (the Lord said) 'to show that my people are like a wall that is out of line.' (7:7-8)

He had a vision also of Bethel's destruction. (Bethel was the Jerusalem of the north – its spiritual capital.)

Call to the North

We don't know exactly when Amos saw his visions, or when he finally became convinced of his calling as God's prophet. All we know is that he felt called to the north. It was in Israel, not in his native Judah, that he was to utter his warnings.

> 'Don't think that your sacrifices will please the Lord,' was his message, 'while you do nothing to relieve the sufferings of the poor. The Lord says, "I hate your religious feasts. I cannot stand them! When you bring me burnt offerings and grain offerings, I will not accept them, nor will I accept the animals you have fattened to bring me as offerings. Stop your noisy songs; I do not want to listen to your harps . . ."' (5:21-23)

One can imagine the effect of this rough-hewn, rough-spoken countryman on Bethel's top people.

None of the rich were spared. Even women were included in his polemic:

Listen to this, you women of Samaria, who grow fat like well-fed cows, who mistreat the weak, oppress the poor, and order your husbands to bring you something to drink. As the Lord is holy, he has promised 'The days will come when they will drag you away with hooks; every one of you will be like a fish on a hook. You will be dragged to the nearest break in the wall and thrown out.' (4:1-3)

How to Read Amos

It may be worth remembering that if the Bible were to be arranged in the order in which it was written, the Book of Amos would most likely be the first book. It is not a difficult book, it would take a quarter of an hour to read its nine chapters.

God's judgement against various nations.

The climax is God's judgement against Israel 1-2

Various discourses   3-6

The visions   7-9

The people to whom Amos was directing his words looked forward to 'The Day of the Lord' (a recurring theme in the Bible). They believed that on this great day God would finally vindicate his chosen people. For Amos however, this day was one of retribution, a *Dies Irae*, a day of wrath.

Relevance to Now

With at least one quarter of our world's present inhabitants going to bed very hungry every evening, while most of us in the western world can spend freely on luxuries, the relevance of Amos's words to our present situation is more than obvious.

His contemporaries took no notice of Amos's warnings. Within thirty years their life of luxury was ended: their country devastated; they were in exile. Will our end be any better?

THE BOOK OF OBADIAH

The brief Book of Obadiah is one of those disturbing parts of the Old Testament which leave you wondering why it is there at all. Vengeance, and delight at the downfall of enemies, are natural enough emotions. But the Bible is about God. How can it show God in so human a way? The background for this short book of poems may help us to understand this problem a little.

When the Babylonians captured Jerusalem in 587 BC, and destroyed it, there were several small nations which were delighted by the humiliation of the Hebrew people. They were the neighbouring states which for long had resented the prosperity, and sometimes the rule, of the Hebrew kings and their people. Prominent in their bitterness were the people of Edom, whose country lay south of the Dead Sea. They seized the chance to help the Babylonians as Jerusalem was reduced to rubble, and extended their own boundaries into Judah.

The Book of Obadiah therefore looks forward to the time when Edom in its turn will be conquered and its people will suffer as the Hebrews had suffered. Then they will realize that God does not allow any injustice to remain unpunished, even when it is committed under the wing of a power as great as Babylon.

It is a harsh way of stating such a hope, expressed by people who were deeply conscious of what their own nation had suffered. The author of this book is using the language of his times. It is a condemnation of all such suffering by one nation at the hands of another. If God really does care for people, people of any nation, he will eventually assert his authority over all his world, and see that its wrongs are put right.

The Man Who Said 'No!'

THE BOOK OF JONAH

If the authors of the forty-six books comprising the Old Testament had submitted their writings to a competition, the anonymous author of the Book of Jonah would surely have won a prize for wit. Even the choice of name for the anti-hero, a mean-minded preacher who hated foreigners, a bigot who showed not the least spark of gratitude, displays something of the author's sense of fun. For 'Jonah' means 'Dove'!

Bigoted Hebrew

God had asked Jonah to preach to the Assyrians living in Nineveh so that they would be converted to God's mercy and forgiveness. No one, in a Jew's estimation, was further from God's mercy than the hated Assyrians. Jonah couldn't believe that God would forgive the people of Nineveh. He tried to run away from God, and jumped on board a ship bound for somewhere quite different. The storm, the sailors' realization that Jonah's presence on board may have provoked it, the whale, the odd arrival on the shore, the surprising and immediate conversion of the Ninevites, Jonah's disgust at God's forgiveness of this hated people – all this is told vividly and with brevity. It is a pity that people have been so preoccupied with the question 'Did a whale really swallow Jonah?' that they have lost sight of the point of the parable. For that's what the Book of Jonah obviously is – a parable. We could as well ask of the Good Samaritan story – 'How much money did the traveller lose?' 'Was he insured?' 'What were the names of the ones who passed by?' Instead we ask, 'What is this story telling me today?'

What an Ass!

Jonah is chosen by the author as a cartoon of the whole Jewish race of his time. The time after the Exile was characterized by a feeling not only of Jewish racial superiority, but a narrow small-mindedness. The author of Jonah very adroitly tells the story of this petty preacher so that a person hearing the story would smile and say 'What an ass Jonah was', only to realize as the story comes to an end that he was that man. One need hardly add that people of every age are liable to religious and racial prejudice. To think that Jonah has nothing to teach us today would be proof enough of that.

THE BOOK OF MICAH

There is something fascinating about a prediction which comes true. Perhaps it satisfies our wish that we could see into the future. What a terrible gift that would be, if we really knew everything that was going to happen to us!

Micah is famous for a prediction he made about the Messiah. In chapter 5 he says that Bethlehem, the home town of the smallest of the Hebrew tribes, would be the birthplace of the saviour sent by God. Bethlehem was the place where King David was born. The Messiah, wrote Micah, would be a ruler even greater than David, who would give his people security and peace, and rule them with justice.

The people of Micah's time had need of such reassurance. The most ruthless military power in the whole history of the Middle East, the Assyrians, was taking over Palestine. They were determined to control the great international roads which thrust through the desert to Egypt, passing through Palestine on their way. The Assyrians would not hesitate to crush any nation which hindered their advance. The northern Hebrew kingdom, Israel, dared to resist the Assyrians. Micah and his fellow citizens of the southern kingdom, Judah, watched helplessly as the Assyrians annihilated their northern brethren and destroyed Samaria, the northern capital.

Indeed, the southern Hebrew king had invited the Assyrians to perform their dreadful crime, and had made an unholy alliance with them.

The Dangers of Prosperity

Little wonder that Micah looked to God for a new king, a holy ruler, who would save his people from the corrupt and avaricious people who ruled them and cheated them. The poor and the honest were attacked from all sides. Merchants used dishonest weights, judges were bribed to give wrong judgement, money-lenders charged high interest rates and collected their debts ruthlessly. Even the priests and official prophets were consumed by greed.

What hope was there for the nation if God did not act swiftly? The nation had a high vocation, said Micah. It was nothing less than to be the hope of the world. The Hebrews were to be a great banner flying on a hilltop, so that all people would know where to go to find God. When the Hebrews ignored that vocation, and forgot that they had been chosen by God for a special purpose, they must be punished. Yet a remnant would always survive, a holy seed, to bear witness to God and bear holy fruit for the future. It is no accident that Micah's teaching is so similar to that of Isaiah, for both men taught at much the same time and throughout the same dramatic events of history.

Micah, like Isaiah, was called to teach his people at the height of their prosperity. Trade and clever political manoeuvring had made the Hebrew people wealthy, and concentrated the wealth into the hands of a few. To bring people back to God at such times was particularly difficult, when so many of the people with influence were corrupted by the wealth they had acquired.

The situation is remarkably like that of the western nations today, obsessed by their economic difficulties yet with so much wealth flowing through them. Micah's message makes uncomfortable reading.

A Tyrant's End

THE BOOK OF NAHUM

There is a terrible satisfaction about the fall of a detested tyrant, and such a fall occurred in 612 BC when the Babylonians finally captured Nineveh, the capital city of the Assyrian empire. Nineveh lay far to the east of Palestine, many hundreds of miles from Jerusalem, yet the Hebrews had felt the terror of Assyrian armies.

Even worse, the people of Jerusalem had betrayed their brethren and their God for fear of the Assyrian invaders. More than a century earlier the southern Hebrews had thrown in their lot with the Assyrians, and had then watched as the Assyrians marched their northern Hebrew brethren away to slavery and oblivion. The Assyrian religion was given pride of place in the Temple in Jerusalem. The Hebrew kings ruled their people as puppets of Nineveh.

Nahum's poems are songs of exultant triumph over the defeated Assyrians and their ruined city. At last, they had received the treatment they so often meted out to others. In a harsh age, such a defeat was seen as evidence of God's power. The enemies of God's people are themselves overthrown. God's justice has triumphed.

A later, anonymous prophet would express another point of view in the story of Jonah. Jonah was sent to convert Nineveh and, in the story, was angry with God when the Assyrians responded. Nahum would have been on the side of Jonah!

THE BOOK OF HABAKKUK

The Bible is full of vivid images, which touch the imagination and linger in the memory.

Such a moment occurs in Habakkuk, when the prophet compares himself to a watchman, gazing out from the battlements of a silent, sleeping city. But Habakkuk is not watching for an enemy who might catch the city unawares, he is waiting patiently and humbly for God to reveal himself to him, so that he can pass on the message to his people.

Habakkuk hopes that the message will be the answer to an urgent problem. Oppressor replaces oppressor in the shifting history of the Middle East. First it was the Egyptians, who were then defeated by the Assyrians. The Assyrians were then replaced by the Babylonians, and the Babylonians by Habakkuk knows not who. Is there to be no end to the ceaseless round of conquering armies, frightened people, and a land which has no chance to recover its prosperity?

God's Instruments

Why does God do nothing about it? Perhaps the oppressors are God's instruments, thinks Habakkuk, sent by him to punish his disobedient people, or at least allowed to rampage about without hindrance. That would make sense, but the cruelty of the foreign invaders is altogether excessive. The Hebrew God may punish his people, but surely they cannot have deserved such harsh punishment? The situation is bewildering. When enlightenment does come to Habakkuk it is nothing dramatic, but he is ordered to write it and publish it so that everyone can read it, understand it and remember it.

It is simply that the upright man has nothing to fear. His righteousness will guarantee him his life.

For the rest, Habakkuk condemns everyone who finds his security in the shifting and transitory values of wealth. Such avarice is as greedy as the grave, as insatiable as death. So exploitation, ambition, cruelty and injustice are all to be punished. They give only false security. Only righteousness endures.

The book ends with a heartfelt song of confidence in God. The watchman remains faithfully at his post, confident that the darkness will end and that righteousness will bring its sure reward.

Searching by Torchlight

THE BOOK OF ZEPHANIAH

If the hour before the dawn seems the darkest and weariest hour of the night, so must the time immediately before a great reform seem the most hopeless time of all.

Such a time belongs to Zephaniah. For three-quarters of a century the Hebrew people lay in the grip of corrupt, ineffective or immature rulers. Every kind of terrible practice found its supporters, even human sacrifice. Injustice and oppression flourished where no sound religion buttressed the laws to protect the weak and the poor.

In fact, although Zephaniah did not know it, a young king named Josiah would sweep away the corruption of his kingdom as soon as he was old enough to wield power confidently. He would renew the Covenant and dedicate his people afresh to God. The old Hebrew religion would be the sole worship again in the Temple in Jerusalem. There would be a new revision of the nation's laws, to show how God's love could be the true basis of justice. The people of God would find their security in their God again.

Torchlight

Meanwhile Zephaniah felt that God could only punish. God would go through the dark places of Jerusalem with torchlight to expose and to punish the complacent rich.

One of Zephaniah's poems, about the wrath which 'the day of God' would bring, inspired a medieval poet to write the *Dies Irae*. It is a black picture of terror and despair for all who have turned their backs on God's love and justice during their lifetime. Yet, as so often in the prophets, Zephaniah ends with deeply moving poems of hope and renewal. Then Jerusalem will ring with shouts of joy as the faithful remnant experiences the freedom of God's salvation.

It is to be a renewal which transforms the hearts and minds of those who experience it. There are hints, here, that the God who saves them is also the Creator who can produce in his people the perfection he expects of them.

THE BOOK OF HAGGAI

Anyone who has started a new enterprise, and persisted with it, knows when the real danger comes.

The real test does not come at the beginning, when the challenge is fresh and hopes are high. It comes a little later, when the first excitement has worn off and there seems no end to the difficulties. The prophet Haggai came on to the scene at just such a moment for the Hebrew people.

Exile

The nation had spent 50 years in exile. During those years its capital city, Jerusalem, had lain in ruins and its land was all but deserted.

Then the new rulers of the Middle East, the Persians, gave the exiles permission to return home again. Carrying the treasures back to their looted Temple, and financed by Persian funds, a party of Hebrews had returned to rebuild the nation in its homeland. Soon their enthusiasm waned as difficulties pressed in on them. Harvests failed. They were tactless with the neighbouring people who offered to help them, and naturally enough their neighbours turned against them. They ran out of money. Everything they did seemed to go wrong.

Haggai put his finger on the central problem. The enthusiasm of the returning exiles had been fuelled by religious motives. They knew they were the holy people of God, returning to Palestine to make it a centre of inspiration for all the world. Yet they had abandoned work on the new Temple in Jerusalem. The site had been cleared and the materials gathered, but the new walls had not risen above the foundations. No wonder that enthusiasm had died away, if the people had no Temple. There was nothing to inspire them and keep alive their ideals. The new Jerusalem needed the Temple as a vivid symbol, or the vision would fade.

Priorities

Haggai urged the people to look to the real source of their strength, and put the Temple at the head of their priorities for building. Then they would find that the rest of their lives would all fall into place and make sense. Years before, near the beginning of the long Exile, another prophet had given hope to the Hebrews far from home in Babylon. Ezekiel had given them a blueprint for a new Jerusalem, built round a new Temple, and promised that the nation would live again (Ezekiel chapters 37 and 40-48).

Now God had sent another prophet, Haggai, to urge the people to remain loyal to that central truth of their lives. Worship of God must be the foundation on which they built the new Jerusalem, so that God's power would nurture every part of the new nation's life. There is a fascinating and intriguing detail in this prophet's brief book. Haggai refers to a leader named Zerubbabel, who was a descendant of King David. Did these pioneers of the new nation hope to restore the line of kings which David had begun? Those kings had failed fifty years earlier and the capital had been destroyed as a result. If the new pioneers meant those kings to continue their intention did not last, for it was the high priest who emerged as the ruler of the new nation.

Perhaps the change was necessary if religion was to receive first priority in the nation's life.

Visions of Hope

THE BOOK OF ZECHARIAH

The prophet Zechariah was teaching the Hebrew people during the stirring and frustrating years which followed the Exile of the Hebrews in Babylon. For fifty years Jerusalem and its Temple had lain in ruins while its citizens were in exile in Babylon. Then the Babylonians had been overthrown by the Persians, and King Cyrus of Persia had sent back to Jerusalem any of the Hebrews who wished to return.

At first they had been full of enthusiasm, but difficulties had quickly dashed their early hopes. They abandoned the work of rebuilding the Temple. First the prophet Haggai and then Zechariah tried to restore their enthusiasm.

International Confusion

Zechariah seized on a period of international confusion. In 522 BC the reigning Persian emperor, Cambyses, committed suicide, and the whole of the Persian empire moved into a period of chaos. One of Cambyses's officers, Darius, defeated the other main claimant to the throne, and rebellion broke out all over the empire. It was two years before Darius had gained complete control again.

The new emperor recorded his success in a great inscription which may still be seen on the rock face at Behistun in Mesopotamia. But the disturbances and rebellions encouraged the returned Hebrews in Jerusalem to believe that the Messianic age had begun, and that this was the 'time of troubles' which they believed would precede God's arrival in his capital city. Jerusalem would become the centre of God's rule over all the world when he had won his final victory over the forces of evil.

Visions

In a series of 'visions' Zechariah seized the opportunity to kindle the returned exiles' devotion to God and encourage them to complete the building of the Temple.

The opening three visions of his book interpret the times as if a Persian cavalry patrol had investigated the situation and reported that the earth was at peace again. Even so, the world powers ('horns') which had troubled the Hebrews must be destroyed, the Temple must be completed, and Jerusalem was to be left without walls. This last command was a particularly vivid symbol, for it showed that the people had full confidence in God as their protector. God was to be a wall of fire all around Jerusalem, and the glory in the midst of the city. The exiles still in Babylon were urged to return to Jerusalem to meet God and share in his triumph.

The fourth and fifth visions show the investiture of Joshua as high priest. There is to be joint rule of the new Messianic kingdom by Joshua and Zerubbabel, who are depicted as olive trees. The remaining three visions show God's victory over evil, and the patrol rides out again to maintain God's rule throughout the world.

Rule by Priests

Interestingly enough, it looks as if Zerubbabel's name has been removed from the text in chapter 6 by a later editor, leaving Joshua the high priest as the sole ruler. Perhaps this marks the point where the people abandoned the possibility of restoring the old Davidic line of kings, of which Zerubbabel was a descendant, leaving the nation to be ruled solely by its priests. The decision would be a natural one, when we remember that the kings had failed the nation so disastrously in the years before the Exile.

The Hebrews in Jerusalem accepted the teaching of Haggai and Zechariah, and pressed on with the work of building the new Temple. The completed Temple was consecrated in 515 BC, twenty-three years after the first Hebrews had returned to Jerusalem from Babylon. The new Temple remained in use until it was replaced by the magnificent building given to the people by Herod the Great five hundred years later.

THE BOOK OF MALACHI

In most editions of the Old Testament this book is printed last, and so it takes on a special significance. For it says in chapter 3 that God will send his messenger to prepare a way before him, when he comes into his Temple to deliver justice. 'Malachi' is simply the Hebrew word for 'my messenger' and it is a mistake to think that this is the name of the prophet who wrote the book. We do not know what his name really was.

Nor is it easy to give it a precise date, except to say that it belongs to the time when the Hebrews were under Persian rule. Hebrew exiles had returned to Palestine, where they were struggling to found the nation again and rebuild the ruined Jerusalem. The Temple had been rebuilt, and worship restored, but the people were only giving God lukewarm worship.

Defective Worship

Worshippers were offering diseased and defective animals in the temple sacrifices. The priests were failing in one of their main duties, that of teaching people the traditions and laws of their faith. Marriages to foreigners were becoming commonplace, and with such mixed marriages alien gods were being worshipped in Jerusalem. Later, Nehemiah and Ezra would bring in legislation to force Hebrews to marry within the nation, and even to divorce wives and disown children when the wife came from another people. But at this stage the people are only urged to avoid dilution of the Hebrew community.

The book ends with a strange promise and warning, that God will send the prophet Elijah again to the people just before the end of the world when the day of judgement comes. Second Kings chapter 2 records that Elijah did not die, but was taken to heaven in a fiery chariot, so it is evident that the people believed he would return in a similar way. According to the Book of Malachi, Elijah will draw families together again so that there will be no judgement on them when God comes to his people.

However strange the details may be, the message of the Book of Malachi is clear. Religion must be the spring and motive of a people if their life is to be one of satisfaction and mutual trust. God alone is the source of the values by which people live, but he can only help his people if they acknowledge his presence and respond to it with whole-hearted devotion.

MAPS

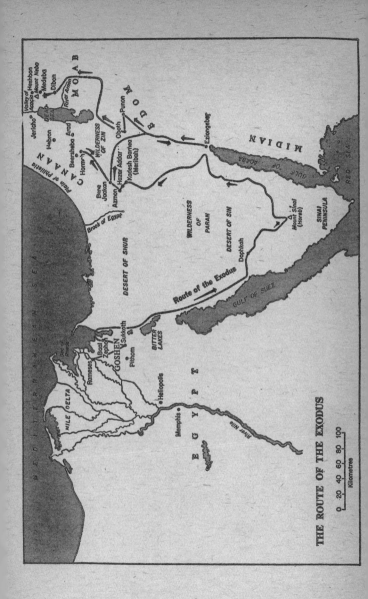

THE ROUTE OF THE EXODUS

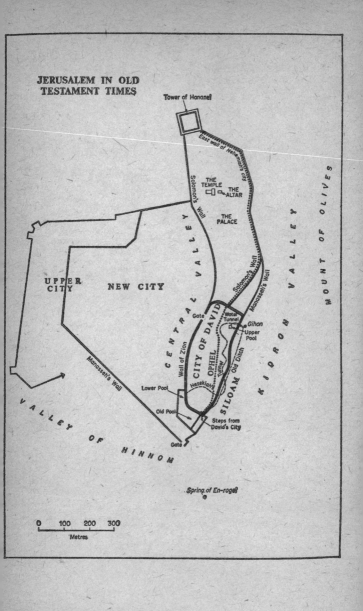

JERUSALEM IN OLD
TESTAMENT TIMES

Tower of Hananel

East wall of Nehemiah's city

Solomon's Wall

THE
TEMPLE
THE
ALTAR

THE
PALACE

Solomon's Wall

Manasseh's Wall

UPPER
CITY

NEW CITY

CENTRAL VALLEY

Gate

City of David

Water
Tunnel

Gihon
Upper
Pool

Wall of Zion

OPHEL

Tunnel

SILOAM

Old Ditch

Hezekiah's

Lower Pool

Old Pool

Steps from
David's City

Gate

KIDRON VALLEY

MOUNT OF OLIVES

Manasseh's Wall

VALLEY OF HINNOM

Spring of En-rogel

0   100   200   300
Metres

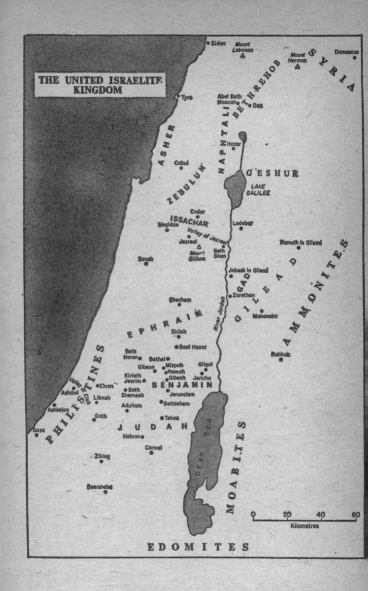

THE UNITED ISRAELITE KINGDOM

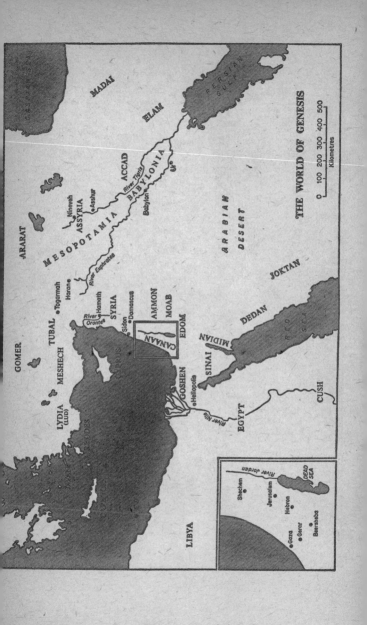

THE WORLD OF GENESIS

0   100 200 300 400 500
Kilometres

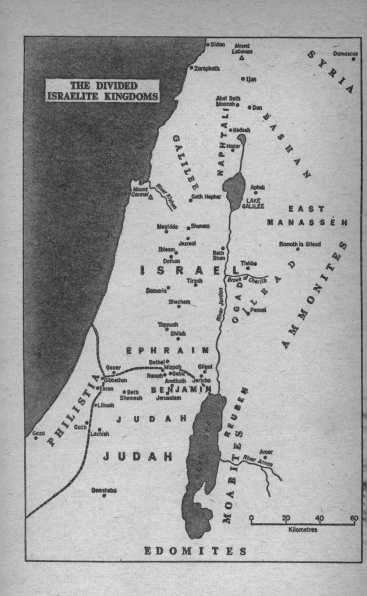

THE DIVIDED
ISRAELITE KINGDOMS

● Sidon
Mount Lebanon △
● Zarephath
Damascus
SYRIA
● Ijon
Abel Beth
Maacah ● Dan
● Kedesh
BASHAN
Hazor
GALILEE
NAPHTALI
Mount Carmel △
River Kishon
Gath Hepher
Aphek
LAKE GALILEE
EAST MANASSEH
Megiddo ● Shunem
Jezreel
Ramoth in Gilead
Ibleam ● Dothan
Beth Shan
Tishbe
I S R A E L
Tirzah
Brook of Cherith
Samaria ●
Shechem
River Jordan
GILEAD
GAD
Penuel
AMMONITES
Tappuah
Shiloh
E P H R A I M
Gezer
Gibbethon
Bethel ● Mizpah Gilgal
Ramah ● Geba ● Jericho
Anathoth
● Ekron
Beth Shemesh
B E N J A M I N
● Libnah
Jerusalem
P H I L I S T I A
J U D A H
REUBEN
DEAD SEA
Gaza ●
Gath ● Lachish
J U D A H
Aroer
River Arnon
MOABITES
● Beersheba
0   20   40   60
Kilometres

E D O M I T E S

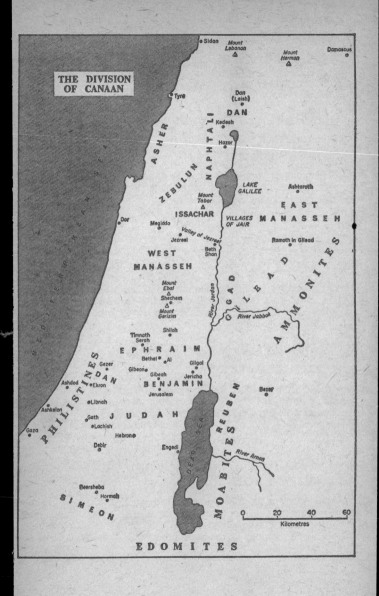

THE DIVISION OF CANAAN

MEDITERRANEAN SEA

Sidon
Mount Lebanon △
Mount Hermon △
Damascus

Tyre

Dan (Laish)

ASHER

DAN

Kedesh

NAPHTALI

Hazor

ZEBULUN

LAKE GALILEE

Ashtaroth

Mount Tabor △

ISSACHAR

EAST MANASSEH

VILLAGES OF JAIR

Dor

Megiddo

Valley of Jezreel

Jezreel

Beth Shan

Ramoth in Gilead

WEST MANASSEH

River Jordan

GILEAD

AMMONITES

Mount Ebal △

Shechem

Mount Garizim △

River Jabbok

GAD

Shiloh

Timnath Serah

EPHRAIM

Gezer

Bethel • Ai

Gilgal

Gibeon

Gibeah

Jericho

DAN

Ashdod

• Ekron

BENJAMIN

Jerusalem

Ashkelon

• Libnah

PHILISTINES

Gath

• Lachish

JUDAH

REUBEN

Bezer

Gaza

Hebron •

DEAD SEA

Debir

Engedi

MOABITES

River Arnon

Beersheba

Hormah •

SIMEON

0   20   40   60

Kilometres

EDOMITES

Also in the Fontana Theology and
Philosophy Series

A Historical Introduction
to the New Testament
ROBERT GRANT

'This splendid book is a New Testament introduction with a
difference . . . All students of the New Testament will welcome
this original and courageous study.'
Professor James S. Stewart

The Historical Geography of the Holy Land
G. ADAM SMITH

'A classic which has fascinated and instructed generations of
students. This masterpiece among the vast literature on the
Bible . . . will continue to delight readers as well as to inform.'
H. H. Rowley

The Dead Sea Scrolls 1947-1969
EDMUND WILSON

'A lucid narrative of the discovery of the scrolls which soon
turns into a learned detective story; then an account of the
excitement, the consternation and the intrigues.'
V. S. Pritchett, New Statesman

The Gospels and the Jesus of History
XAVIER LEON-DUFOUR

'This book is far more than an introduction to the study of
the Gospels. With its detailed study of the Gospels and of the
other New Testament books it is an excellent introduction
to the Christology of the New Testament.' *William Barclay*